KU-061-923

This book and your GCSE course

	AQA A	AQA B	EDEXCEL
Syllabus name	Physical Education	Physical Education	Physical Education
Syllabus number	3581	3582	1827
Modular tests	none	none	none
Terminal papers	1 paper, 2 hrs, 40%	1 paper, 1hr 30mins, 30%	1 paper, 1hr 45 mins, 40%
Coursework	Practical performance 50% Health Related Training Programme 10%	Practical Activities 50% Analytical Investigation 20%	Practical assessment 25% Analysis of performance 10% Final assessment 25%
Physical education/Games	SPECIFICATION REFERENCE NUMBERS		
Major body systems	9.1	9.1	C1, C2, C3, C4, C5
Fitness	9.2	9.2	A2, A3
Training methods and programmes	9.1, 9.2	9.1, 9.2	A4, A5
Skill	9.2	9.2	A3
Measurement in sport	9.2	9.2	A5
Factors affecting performance	9.1, 9.2	9.1, 9.2	A1, A6, B1
Sports related injuries	9.2	9.2	B1, B2
Sport within society	9.3	9.3	A1, A6
Major influences on participation	9.3	9.3	A6
The media and its influence on participation	9.4	9.4	
Organisation of sport	9.3	9.3	
Providers of sport	9.4	9.4	

Visit your awarding body website for full details of your course or download your complete GCSE specific

STAY YOUR COURSE!

Use these pages to get to know your course

- *Make sure you know your exam board*
- *Check which specification you are doing*
- *Know how your course is assessed:*
  - *what format are the papers?*
  - *how is coursework assessed?*
  - *how many papers?*

OCR PE	OCR Games	WJEC	NICCEA
Physical Education	Physical Education (Games)	Physical Education	Physical Education
1970	1971	197	-
none	none	none	none
1 paper, 1hr 45 mins, 40%	1 paper, 1hr 45 mins, 40%	2 papers Paper 1: 1 hr 30mins, 20% Paper 2: 1 hr 30mins, 20%	1 paper, 1 hr 30mins, 30%
Practical Performance and Analysis of one activity 60%	Practical Performance and Analysis of one game 60%	Physical Activities 60%	Individual performance 50% Analysis and improvement 20%
5.1	5.1	B.5.4	✓
5.2	5.2	B.5.1, B.5.3	✓
5.1, 5.2	5.1, 5.2	B.5.1	✓
5.1	5.1	B.5.5	✓
5.2	5.2	B.5.3	✓
5.1, 5.2	5.1, 5.2	B.5.4	✓
5.3	5.3	B.5.4	✓
5.1	5.1	B.5.2	✓
5.1	5.1	B.5.2	✓
5.1	5.1	B.5.2	✓
5.1	5.1	B.5.2	✓
5.1	5.1	B.5.2	✓
	Throughout the book this specification is labelled OCR G		

Preparing for the examination

Although the Physical Education and Games courses offered at GCSE level are essentially practical subjects, the **examination is worth 40% of the total available marks** for the final grade award (30% in the case of AQA). The exam is therefore an important part of the course.

Your revision time before the exam is important. It is during this period that you will be able to identify the parts of the course that you know and understand and the parts that you are less confident about.

A revision programme is a big undertaking and cannot be started too early. Some careful planning and organisation and use of this Study Guide should pay dividends at exam time.

Preparing a revision programme

You should already have covered all the course units to be studied. All that is now needed is to refresh your memory and add to it. You should devise a realistic revision programme that will be effective. Your programme should:

- identify what you already know about a topic
- show what areas you need to concentrate on
- allocate time in the most effective way

Think of your revision programme as you would a physical training programme. It should contain a mixture of:

- simple revision sessions (light training sessions), followed by
- heavy learning sessions (hard intensive training), with
- built-in rest days

How this book can help

Revise GCSE PE Study Guide can help because:

- It covers all the essential topics in your PE/games scheme
- It contains Progress Check questions, sample GCSE questions and exam practice questions
- It includes all the answers to sample and practice questions, with advice from experienced examiners
- The table on pages 4–5 will give you a quick reference to the requirements for you examination
- Margin comments and highlighted key points will focus your attention on the most important aspects of the course

Four ways to improve your grade

1 When revising

- Choose a work place where you will not easily be distracted.
- Try to ensure that you get enough sleep.
- Make a realistic estimate of what you can cover in any one week.
- Divide your time into 30- or 40-minute slots with short recovery breaks.
- Choose to revise a topic that you can complete in a set time.
- Use exam questions to highlight what you know and what you are not sure of.
- Be prepared to go back and revise a topic for a second or third time if necessary.
- Ask your teacher if you cannot understand a topic – they are there to help!

2 Learning and remembering

You might want to use one or more of the following memory aids.

- **Repetition** – by writing or saying something aloud over and over you can often learn it 'parrot fashion'. (However, this method has drawbacks as you might not always understand what you remember.)
- **Mnemonics** – the use of a word whose letters remind you of important information. For example, **RICE** = rest, ice, compression, elevation. If you make up your own mnemonic, use a word that is distinctive and easy to remember.
- **Flow diagrams** – start with a key word and link it with lines to other words. The lines may radiate like a sun, go up and down like a ladder, or link words in a circle. See Chapter 2 Fig 2.1 or Chapter 4 Fig 4.5 for examples.
- **Prompt cards** – these are best made by yourself and should contain only the key facts or words in a topic. They help jog your memory.

3 When preparing for the exams

- Give yourself plenty of practice in reading exam questions. You must understand terms like **discuss**, **explain** and **describe**.
- **Practise answering exam questions** as often as you can – this will help prepare you for the real thing.
- **Note the mark allocation** for a particular question. This will indicate how many facts are required in the answer.
- Have a **positive attitude** when you go into the exam.

4 When answering exam questions

- **Read** the questions carefully.
- **Write** clearly and legibly.
- **Remember** that extra marks are given for good spelling, punctuation and grammar.

Tables of norms relating to tests described

Reminder – these tables are an indication only of levels attained. Incorrect test protocol can affect their validity.

A1 Rating table for suppleness

RATING	SHOULDER LIFT	SIT AND REACH	TRUNK EXTENSION
VERY GOOD	36+	10+	50+
GOOD	25+	5+	40+
FAIR	20+	0+	30+
POOR	15+	–5	20+
All scores are in cm			

A2 Rating table for strength

RATING	STANDING LONG JUMP	STANDING HIGH JUMP	SIT-UPS
VERY GOOD	190+	65+	25+
GOOD	170+	60+	20+
FAIR	150+	50+	16+
POOR	130+	40+	14+
Scores for Standing Long Jump and Standing High Jump in cm			

A3 Rating table for cardiovascular endurance

RATING	STEP TEST	12-minute RUN	
		male	female
VERY GOOD	90+	2600+	2200+
GOOD	80+	2400+	2000+
FAIR	65+	2200+	1800+
POOR	50+	2000+	1700+
Scores for 12-minute run in metres			

Factors affecting cardiovascular endurance

- As both the tests described each take several minutes to perform, the attitude of the subject can inflence the outcome.
- The results of the 12-minute run can be affected by the weather.
- If the subjects are tested in groups, they may compete with each other and inflate their scores.

A4 Rating table for agility

TIME IN SECONDS		RATING
male	female	
less than 15.2	less than 17.0	excellent
16.1 – 15.2	17.9 – 17.0	good
18.1 – 16.2	21.7 – 18.0	average
19.3 – 18.2	23.0 – 21.8	fair
more than 19.3	more than 23.0	poor

Chapter

1 Major body systems

The following topics are covered in this chapter:

- ***Skeletal system***
- ***Muscular system***
- ***Circulatory system***
- ***Respiratory system***

1.1 The skeletal system

After studying this section you should be able to:

- ***describe the functions of the skeleton and name the main bones of the body***
- ***describe the main types of joints and know the importance of types of cartilage***

The skeleton

AQA A   AQA B   EDEXCEL   OCR PE   OCR G   NICCEA

The skeleton of the body has **FOUR** main functions.

Table 1.1 Four functions of the skeleton

1 Blood production	this takes place within the cavities of the long bones.
2 Protection	soft tissue and delicate organs of the body, such as the brain, the heart and the lungs, are surrounded by bones.
3 Support	without the skeleton we would not be able to keep our shape. Also, some organs are suspended from bony tissue.
4 Movement	if muscles could not pull on several rigid bones, it would not be possible for us to move.

The skeleton is made up of a large number of bones all joined together.

Recall the names and positions of the major bones of the body.

Fig 1.1 The human skeleton

Cranium
Clavicle (Collar bone)
Scapula (Shoulder blade)
Humerus
Radius
Ulna
Carpals
Metacarpals
Phalanges
Fibula
Tibia
Orbit (houses eye)
Lower jaw
Cervical vertebrae (Neck) 7
Thoracic vertebrae (Ribs) 12
Sternum (Breast bone)
Lumbar vertebrae 5
Pelvic girdle
Sacrum
Coccyx 4
Femur
Patella (Kneecap)
Tarsals
Metatarsals
Phalanges

Numbers in circles refer to the number of vertebrae in that particular area of the spine.

- The **axial** skeleton, around which other bones move, includes the **skull** and the **thoracic vertebrae**.
- The **appendicular** skeleton includes those bones attached directly or indirectly to the axial skeleton. These include the **shoulder and hip girdles**, and the **arms and legs**.

KEY POINT
The skeleton is sub-divided into two main parts:
- **axial**
- **appendicular**

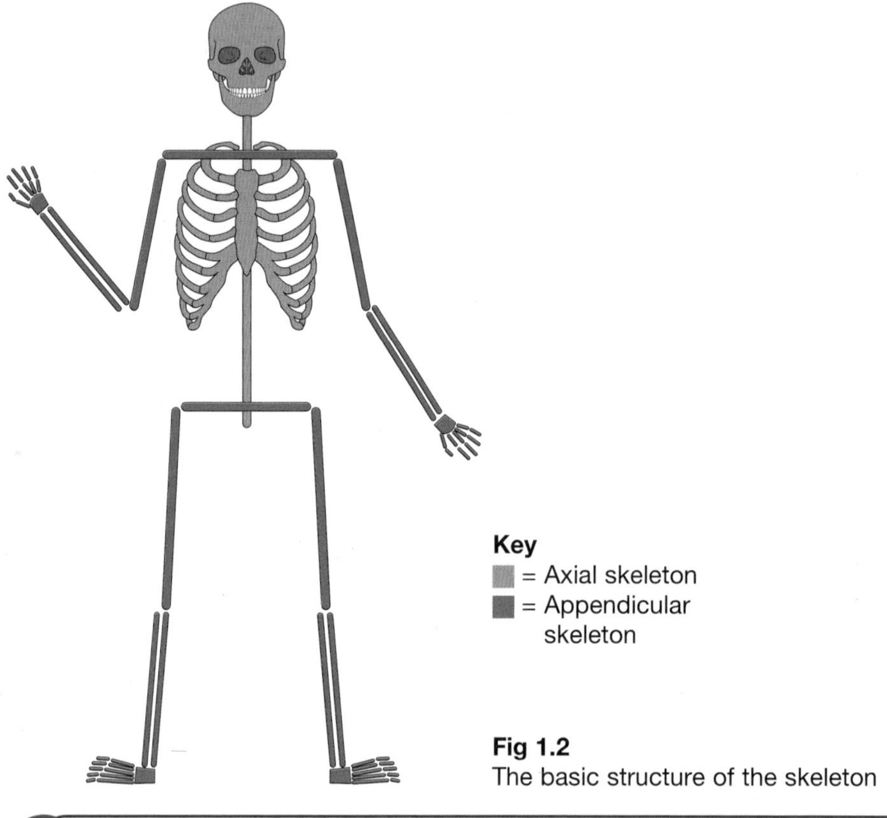

Fig 1.2
The basic structure of the skeleton

KEY POINT
The places where two or more bones meet are called joints.

Joints and cartilage

AQA A AQA B EDEXCEL OCR PE OCR G NICCEA

The major types of joints are listed in Table 1.2. Joint types i to vi are synovial joints (see page 12).

Table 1.2 Types of joints

Type	How strong	Position in body	Range of movement
i ball and socket	very strong	hip/shoulder	full
ii hinge	fairly strong	elbow	limited
iii saddle	fairly weak	base of thumb	limited
iv condyloid	weak	wrist	two ways only
v pivot	fairly strong	neck	rotation only
vi slightly movable	weak	vertebrae (spine)	depends on position
vii immovable		skull sacrum	none none

The range of movement at the joints is shown in Fig 1.3. This, in turn, allows for the movements of the body limbs shown in Fig 1.4.

Fig 1.3 Range of movement at joints

(i) Ball and socket joint
The ball-shaped end of the femur fits into a cup-shaped socket in the pelvis and allows for movement in all directions.

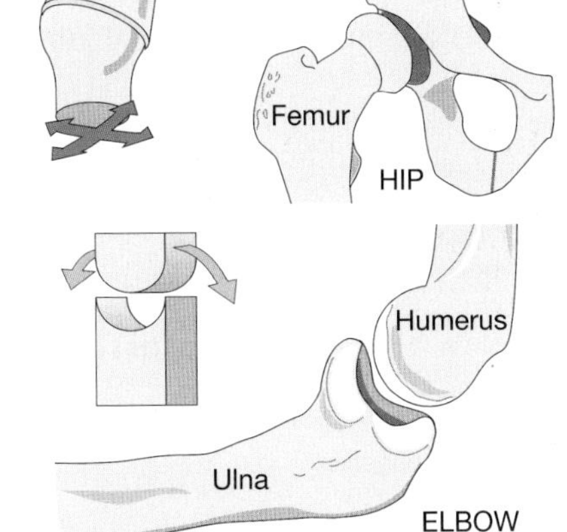

(ii) Hinge joint
Movement is allowed in one plane only.

(iii) Saddle joint
The opposing convex and concave surfaces of the two bones allow movement in two directions.

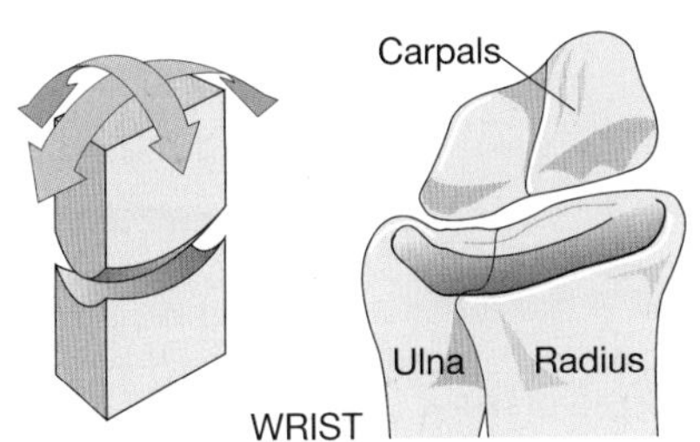

(iv) Condyloid joint
The full convex shape of one bone end fits into the full concave shape of an adjoining bone. This allows for movement in all directions, but ligaments prevent

(v) Pivot joint
In the case of the atlas and axis vertebrae, a circular section of the atlas sits on top of the peg shape of the axis. In the case of the radius and ulna, the radius is held within a fibrous ring attached to the ulna. Both these joints allow rotation to take place.

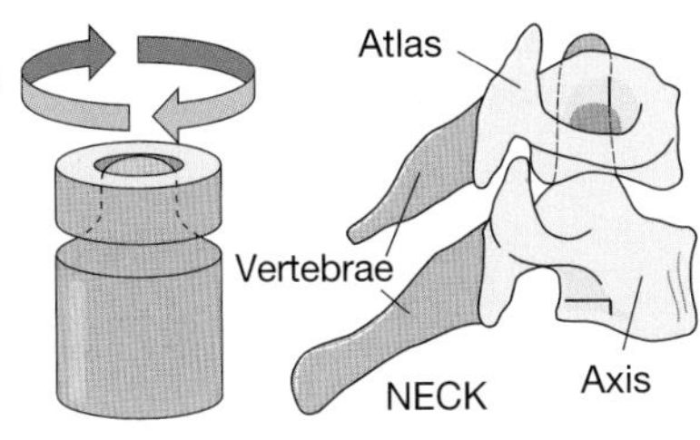

(vi) Slightly movable joint
When the back bends, the joint between two vertebrae moves only a small amount. The disc between the vertebrae is compressed on one side.

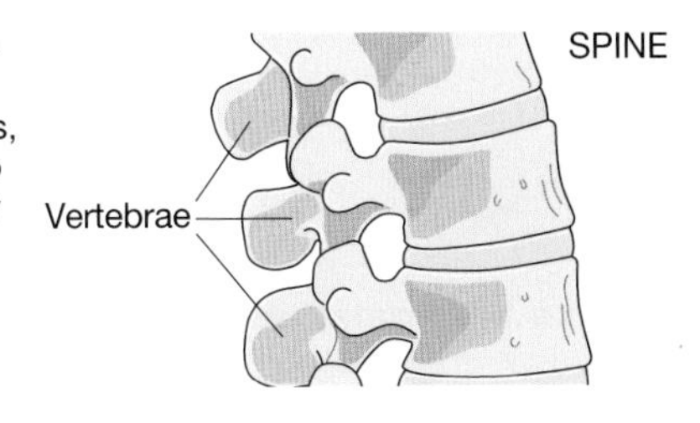

(vii) Immovable joint
The bones have fused together.

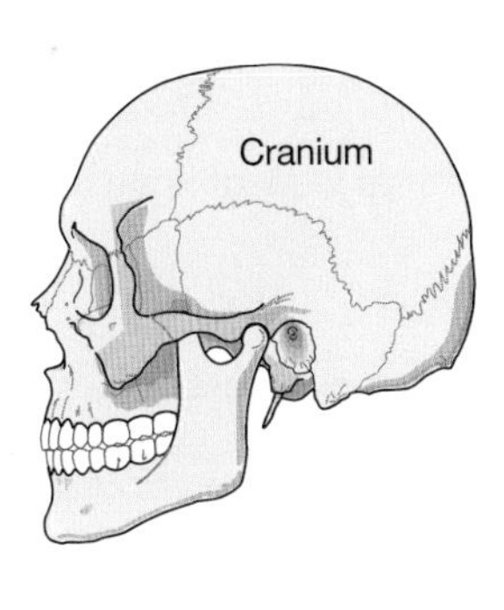

Fig 1.4 Type of movement

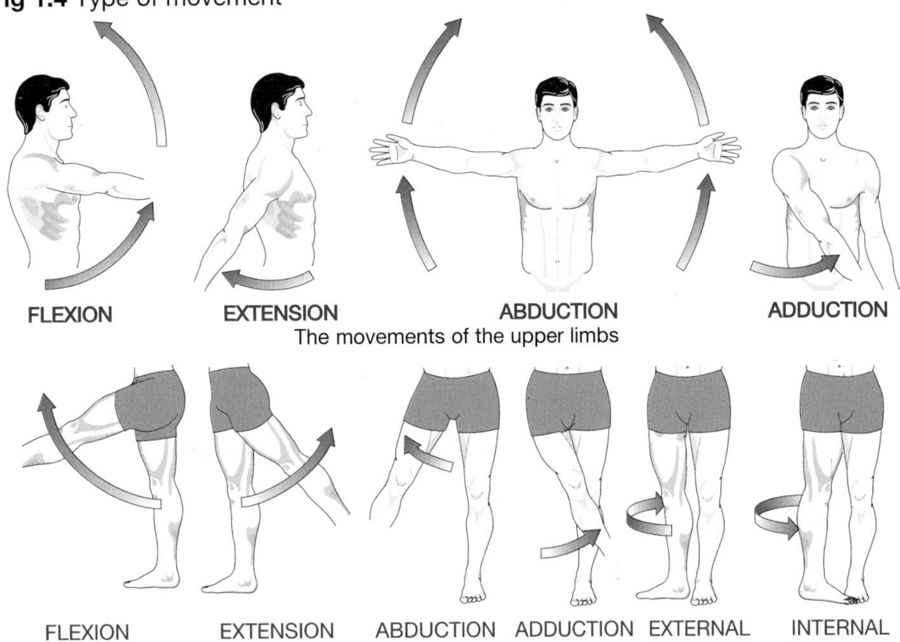

Limb movement away from centre of the body is abduction; limb movement towards the centre of the body is adduction; circular movement or circumduction combines all the movements at the hip.

Do not mix up ligaments and tendons. Ligaments attach bone to bone; tendons attach muscle to bone.

Bones at movable joints are attached to each other by ligaments.

Movable joints are often referred to as **synovial joints**. This is because they are surrounded by a synovial membrane which contains synovial fluid. The fluid acts like the oil in the car engine: it lubricates the joint and helps to maintain movement. The knee joint is a good example of a synovial joint (see Fig 1.5).

Fig 1.5 Structure of the knee joint

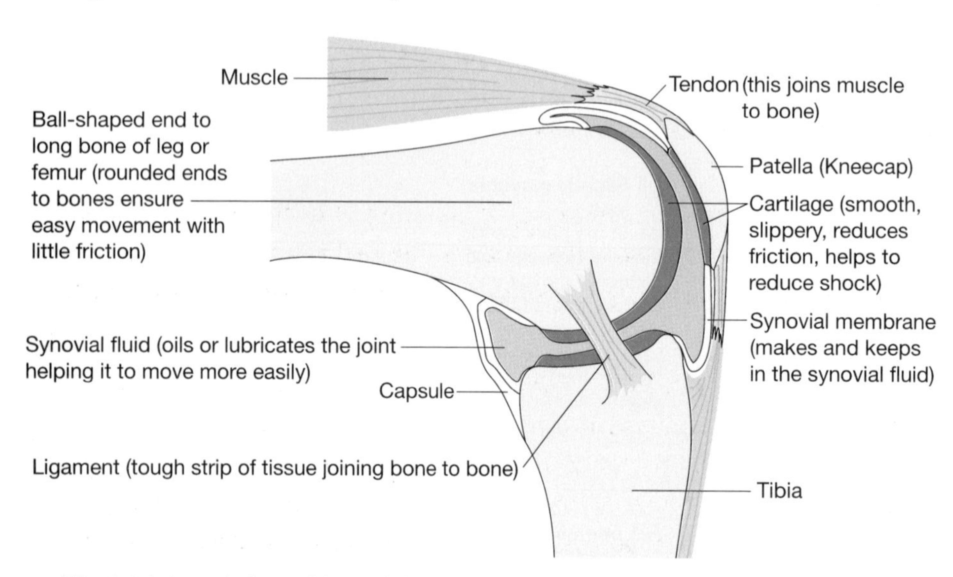

The knee joint also shows the two main types of cartilage found at a joint. These are:

- **articular**
- **menisci**

Articular cartilage is found at the end of the long bones. It is extremely hard, yet smooth and slippery. It protects the ends of the bones from wear.

Menisci (singular meniscus) look like crescent-shaped moons and, although they are attached to the long bones, they come between them. They are made of a softer material and act as shock absorbers between the two long bones (see Fig 1.6).

Fig 1.6 Internal view of knee joint

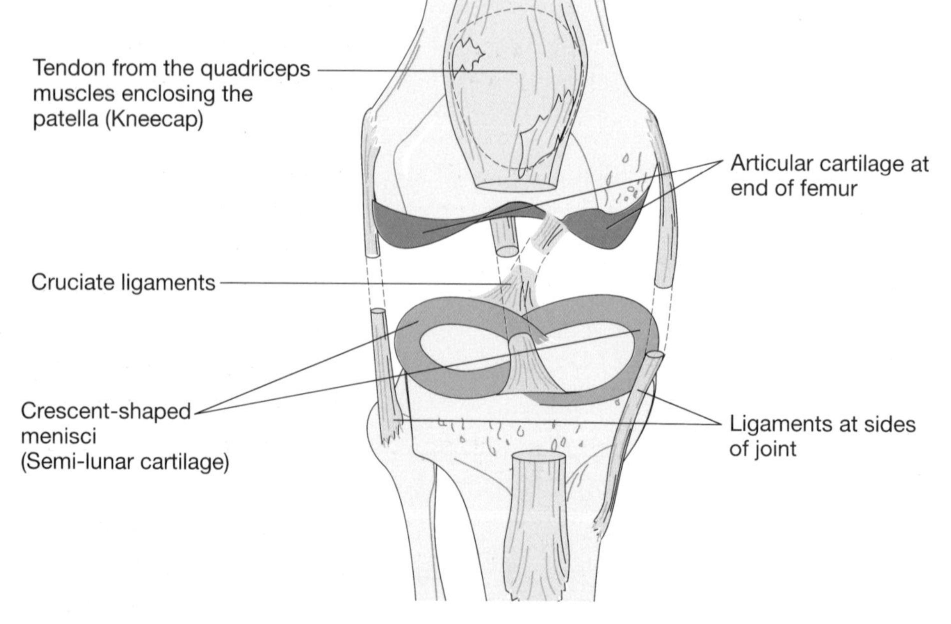

1. List the four major functions of the skeleton.
2. What is the difference between a ligament and a tendon?
3. Explain the terms abduction and adduction.

1. Blood production, protection, support, movement. 2. Ligaments attach bone to bone; tendons attach muscle to bone. 3. Abduction is movement away from the centre of the body; adduction is movement towards the centre of the body.

1.2 The muscular system

After studying this section you should be able to:

- ***describe the three major types of muscle fibre***
- ***describe how the muscles work together***

Muscle fibre

OCR PE
NICCEA

The body has three main types of muscle fibre:

- **cardiac**
- **smooth**
- **skeletal**

Cardiac muscle fibre: this is found only in the heart. It contracts and relaxes continually and its job is to ensure that blood is pumped around the body. The individual fibres of cardiac muscle are inter-twined so that they can pull on each other (see Fig 1.7).

Fig 1.7

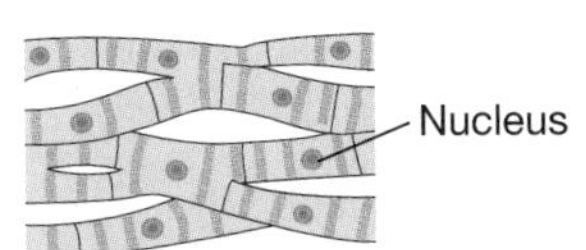

Smooth muscle fibre: this is often called **involuntary** muscle fibre as we have no control over its actions. Smooth muscle fibres make up the walls of certain soft tissues, such as the stomach, bladder and intestines. They allow the walls of these organs to stretch as they become full and return to their original size as they empty. The fibres are laid side by side in layers to make up sheaths of smooth muscle (see Fig 1.8).

Fig 1.8

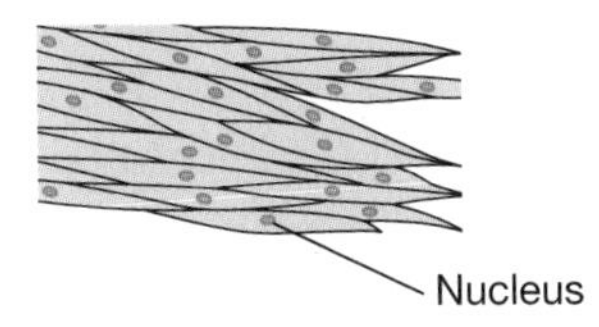

Do not use abbreviations

Fig 1.9 The muscular system

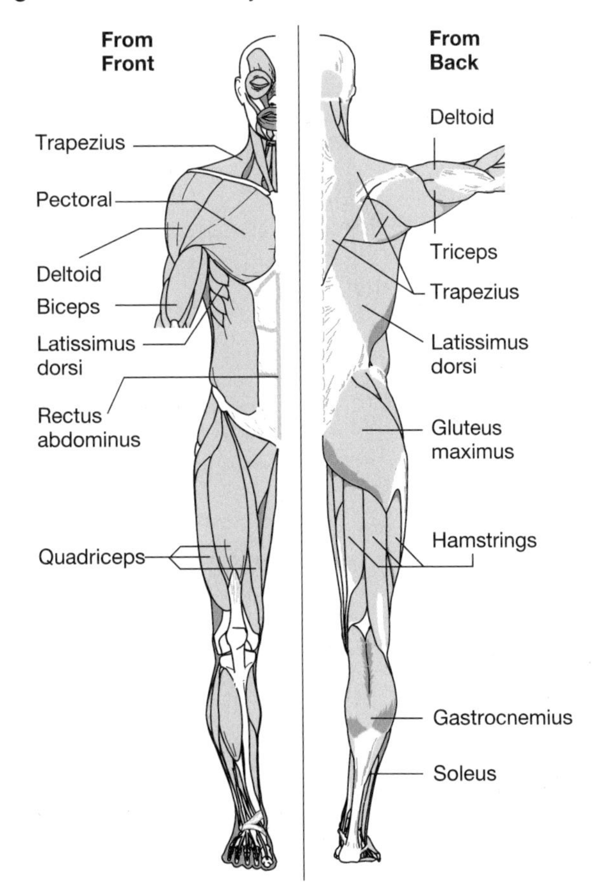

Skeletal muscle fibre: the muscles that contain these fibres are the ones that we use to create movement. These muscles are also called **voluntary** muscles and **striated or striped** muscles: voluntary because we have control over them, so that we can tell them when to contract or relax; striated or striped because under a microscope they have a striped appearance. These skeletal muscles make up the geography or shape of the body (see Fig 1.9).

You should be able to name and place the major skeletal muscle groups of the body.

Fig 1.10 Skeletal muscle fibre

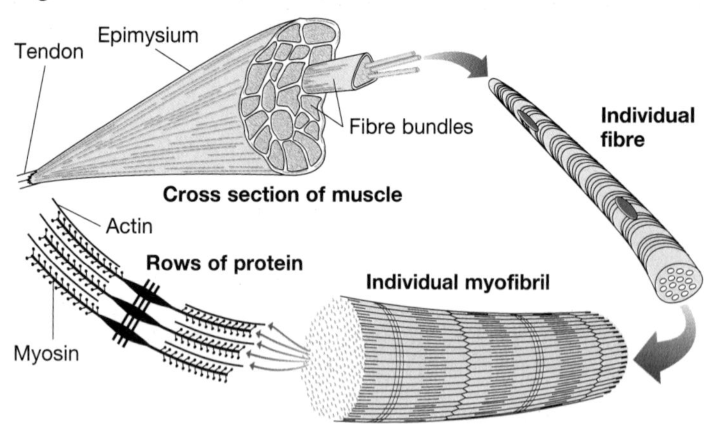

Each muscle contains a number of bundles of fibres, the fibres all lying alongside each other. Each fibre is made up of many much smaller **myofibrils** which, in turn, are made up of strands of protein called **actin** and **myosin**. It is the action of these two proteins sliding together that brings about movement in the whole muscle (see Fig 1.10).

How muscles work

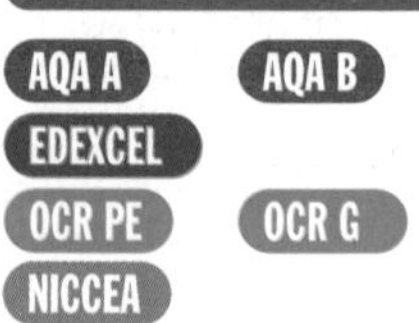

Skeletal muscles are attached to the bones of the skeleton by a connective tissue called a **tendon**. When these muscles contract, they pull on bones at a joint and cause movement. These muscles never work alone: they always work in pairs or groups. As one muscle contracts, another will relax. We often describe these particular skeletal muscles by the work they are doing. For example, a muscle that contracts and causes movement is called an **agonist** or **prime mover**, whilst the muscle that relaxes is called an **antagonist**.

In the case of the elbow, when the biceps contract, the elbow joint closes. This is called **flexion**. At the same time the triceps relax. In this action the biceps are the agonist and the triceps are the antagonist.

Fig 1.11 How muscles work together

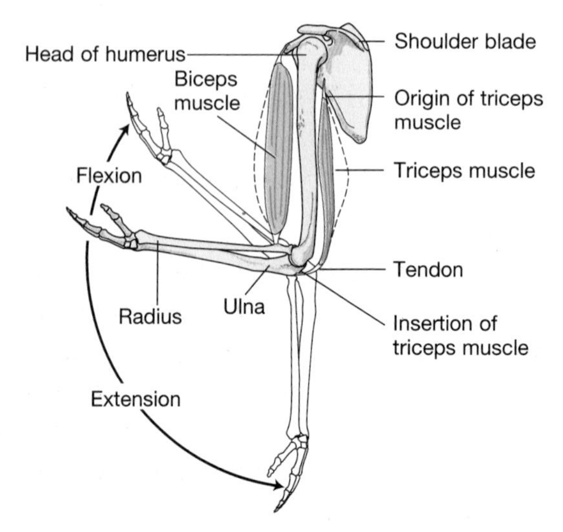

The elbow joint is an example of a hinged joint. It is capable of flexion and extension but not rotation. The dashed lines show the change in shape of the muscles during flexion and extension of the arm.

However, when the triceps contract the elbow joint opens. This is called **extension**. At the same time the biceps relax. In this action the triceps are the agonist and the biceps are the antagonist (see Fig 1.11).

The points where muscles are attached to the bones by tendons are called the points of **origin** and **insertion**. The point of origin is the point of attachment that *does not* move as flexion or extension takes place. The point of insertion is the point of attachment that *does* move during flexion or extension (see Fig 1.11).

Because of the job they do, skeletal muscle fibres are divided into two further muscle groups. These are called **fast twitch** and **slow twitch** fibres. We are all born with the same number of skeletal muscle fibres but we all have a different number of fast or slow twitch fibres. The importance of this is illustrated in Table 1.3.

- Fast twitch fibres are suitable for explosive events such as the shot put or 100 m race.
- Slow twitch fibres are more suited to endurance events such as the marathon.

Table 1.3 Fast and slow twitch fibres

Fast twitch	Slow twitch
shorter	longer
thicker	thinner
contract quickly	contract slowly
exhaust quickly	exhaust slowly

PROGRESS CHECK

1. Explain why smooth muscle fibre is often called involuntary fibre.
2. Where in the body will you find your
   i. deltoids
   ii. gastrocnemius
   iii. gluteus maximus
3. What is the difference between an agonist and an antagonist?

1. We do not have control over the actions of these muscle fibres: they work automatically.
2. i Deltoids - point of shoulder; ii gastrocnemius – back of lower calf; iii gluteus maximus – buttocks. 3. An agonist muscle contracts whilst an antagonist relaxes as a joint moves.

1.3 The circulatory system

LEARNING SUMMARY

After studying this section you should be able to:

- ***identify and describe the main parts of the system***
- ***describe the pathway that blood follows***
- ***describe the make up and function of blood***
- ***describe the effects of exercise on the system***

Parts of the circulatory system

AQA A AQA B EDEXCEL OCR PE OCR G NICCEA

The circulatory system has three main parts:

- the heart that pushes blood around the body
- the blood vessels that carry the blood around the body
- the blood which acts as the transport system of the body

Fig 1.12 Structure of heart showing direction of blood flow

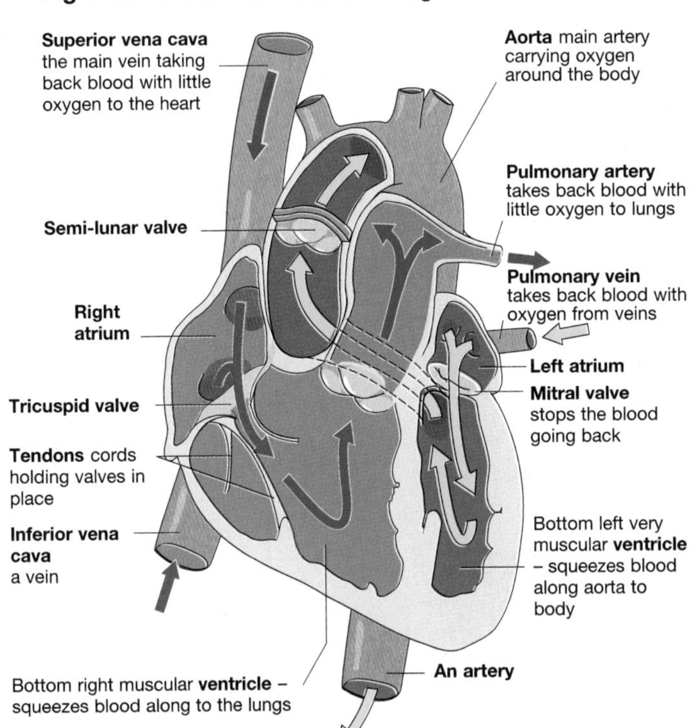

The heart is made up of four distinct chambers and can be described as two muscular pumps working side by side. Each upper chamber is called an **atrium** (plural **atria**) and each lower chamber is called a **ventricle**. The blood enters the heart through an atrium and leaves via a ventricle (see Fig 1.12).

Be able to draw a representation of the heart.

KEY POINT

The continual contraction and relaxation of the heart means that blood does not flow evenly into the arteries. It is forced out of the heart in surges, which are called the pulse beat of the heart.

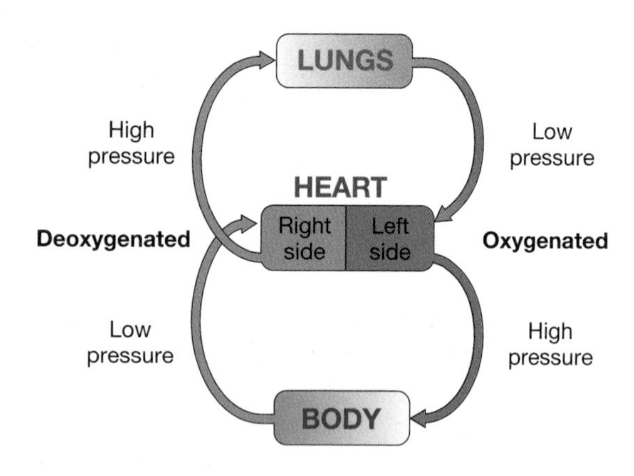

Fig 1.13 Blood pathway round the body

Blood pathway

When blood leaves the heart it travels to either the lungs or around the body. The blood on the right side looking out from the page is deoxygenated blood. That on the left side contains oxygen (see Fig 1.13).

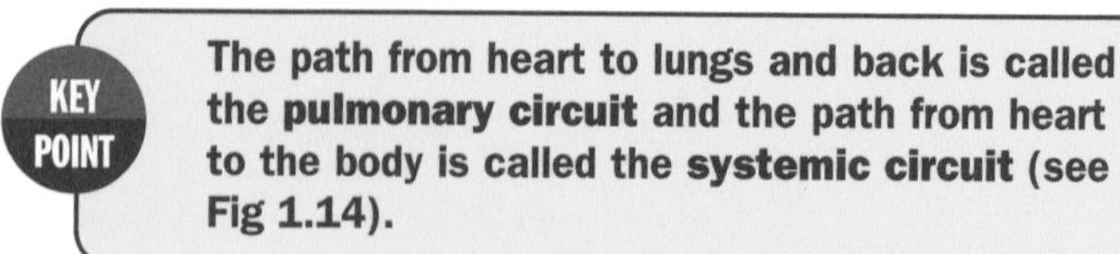

KEY POINT

The path from heart to lungs and back is called the pulmonary circuit and the path from heart to the body is called the systemic circuit (see Fig 1.14).

Be able to draw and describe each of these two circuits.

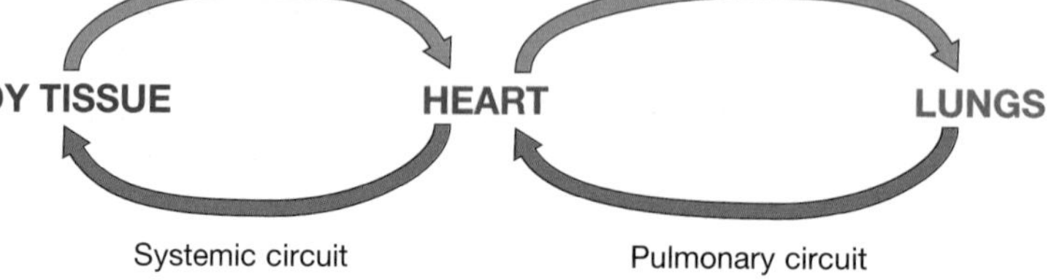

Fig 1.14 Pulmonary and systemic circuits side by side

The blood is forced round the body by the heart through a number of different types of blood vessels. Those taking the blood away from the heart are called **arteries**, and those bringing it back to the heart are called **veins**. Arteries and veins are linked to each other by very small **capillaries** (see Fig 1.15).

Always describe the pathway as though you are lying on your back looking up through the page.

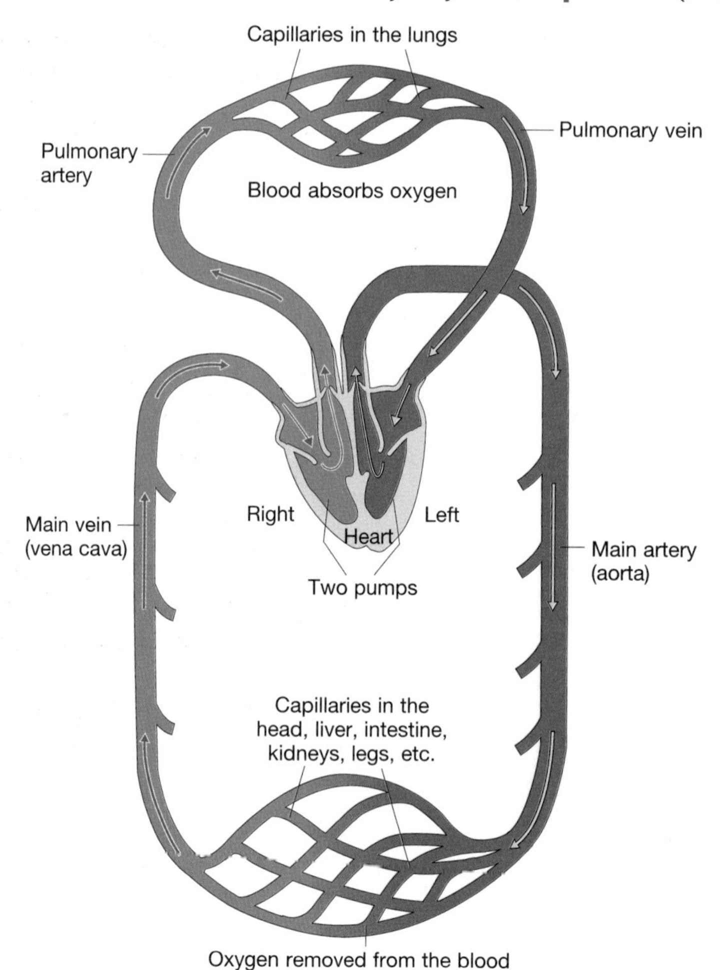

Fig 1.15 The circulation of blood (seen from the front of a person)

Make up and function of blood

AQA A AQA B
EDEXCEL
OCR PE OCR G
NICCEA

Whole blood is made up of **plasma**, **red cells**, **white cells** and **platelets**.

Remember that the cells are transported round the body in the plasma.

Table 1.4 Parts of the blood

WHOLE BLOOD	
PLASMA:	mainly water – contains **fibrinogen**, a protein that is converted to **fibrin** during clotting, and acts as the transportation system
RED CELLS:	bi-concave discs containing an oxygen-carrying substance called **haemoglobin**, which is reddish in colour
WHITE CELLS:	these are of two main types, **phagocytes** and **lymphocytes**, all irregular in shape – they help to fight toxins and bacteria
PLATELETS:	tiny cells without a nucleus, containing an **enzyme** which reacts when exposed to air and aids clotting

Function of blood

KEY POINT

The main functions of blood are **transportation** and **protection.**

You should be able to describe the transportation function of blood.

Table 1.5 Materials transported by blood

Oxygen	**From the lungs to all body tissue** Oxygen combines with the haemoglobin of the red cells in the capillaries of the lungs. The haemoglobin gives up the oxygen to body tissue such as the stomach or muscles when required.
Carbon dioxide	**From all tissues to the lungs** Carbon dioxide forms a solution with the plasma which, when it reaches the lungs, gives up the carbon dioxide so that it can be exhaled.
Nutrients	**From the small intestine to all parts of the body** These are carried in solution form within the plasma.
Heat	**From the muscles to all parts of the body** When the muscles work they get hot. As the blood moves round the body it transports this heat to the cooler parts, so that an even temperature can be maintained. If the body becomes very hot, the blood fills capillaries near the surface of the skin so that heat can escape from the body.
Waste products	**From all body tissue to the kidneys** Any waste product formed within the body is filtered through the kidneys so that it can be excreted.

Table 1.6 Body protection by blood

Antitoxins	These are produced by the lymphocytes to fight toxins (poisons) that might enter the body.
Antibodies	These are produced by the lymphocytes to fight disease and are kept in the blood stream. They give immunity to certain illnesses.
Destruction	This is done by phagocytes. When bacteria causes a threat to the body, the phagocytes attach themselves to, and 'eat' the harmful organisms.
Clotting	This is activated by the platelets. When a blood vessel is cut, the platelets combine together forming a temporary plug to stop immediate blood loss. The enzymes in the platelets react with the air and cause the fibrinogen from the plasma to change into thread-like fibres of fibrin. These form a mesh which seals the wound and prevents the entry of harmful bacteria. We see this mesh of fibres as a scab on a cut.
Repair	The blood acts as a transport system for nutrients and other materials that are needed to repair damaged tissue. This might be the repair of a cut on the body surface or the repair of broken capillaries that have formed a bruise under the surface of the skin.

Be able to describe the protective function of the blood.

Effects of exercise

The effects that exercise has on the circulatory system depend on the type of physical activity performed, the intensity of the activity and the length of time spent on the activity.

Muscles get priority for blood during exercise.

Table 1.7 Main changes brought about during short-term physical activity

Heart	• increase in pulse rate • increase in blood pressure
Blood	• more brought into use • diverted from the soft organs • transports heat from the muscles to the body surface

Be able to differentiate between the effects of short-term and long-term effects on the heart and blood.

Table 1.8 Main effects of long-term high intensity activity

Heart	• increase in size • resting rate becomes lower • stroke volume is increased (pumps more blood with each stroke) • returns to resting rate faster after activity • helps prevent onset of coronary artery disease
Blood	• number of red blood cells is increased, improving potential to transport oxygen • supply to muscle fibres is improved, so more capillaries are available for blood to flow through • return of deoxygenated blood to heart is improved

PROGRESS CHECK

1. Explain how the blood helps to stop the body from overheating during exercise.
2. Name the chambers of the heart.
3. Explain how the blood prevents loss through an open wound.
4. Where do the pulmonary and systemic circuits lead to from the heart?

1. It transports heat to the cooler parts of the body, often near the surface of the skin. This is why we go red when we are hot. 2. Left and right atria; left and right ventricle.
3. Blood clots at the site of an open wound. Enzymes from the platelets react with air and cause the fibrinogen to change into fibrin. These fibres form a mesh to seal the wound.
4. Pulmonary circuits go to the lungs; systemic circuits go to the body tissue.

1.4 The respiratory system

LEARNING SUMMARY

After studying this section you should be able to:

- ***describe the respiratory system and the breathing mechanism***
- ***describe the effects of exercise on the system***
- ***explain how oxygen and carbon dioxide are diffused***

The respiratory system and breathing

AQA A · AQA B · EDEXCEL · OCR PE · OCR G · NICCEA

The three main parts of the respiratory system are:

- **nasal passages**
- **windpipe**
- **lungs**

The lungs are found within the **thoracic cavity** (chest), protected all round by the ribs and at the bottom by a strong elastic sheath called the **diaphragm** (see Fig 1.16).

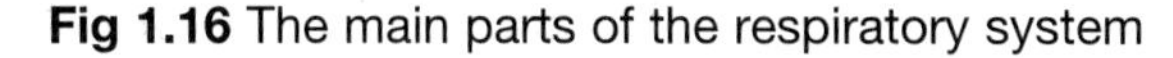

Fig 1.16 The main parts of the respiratory system

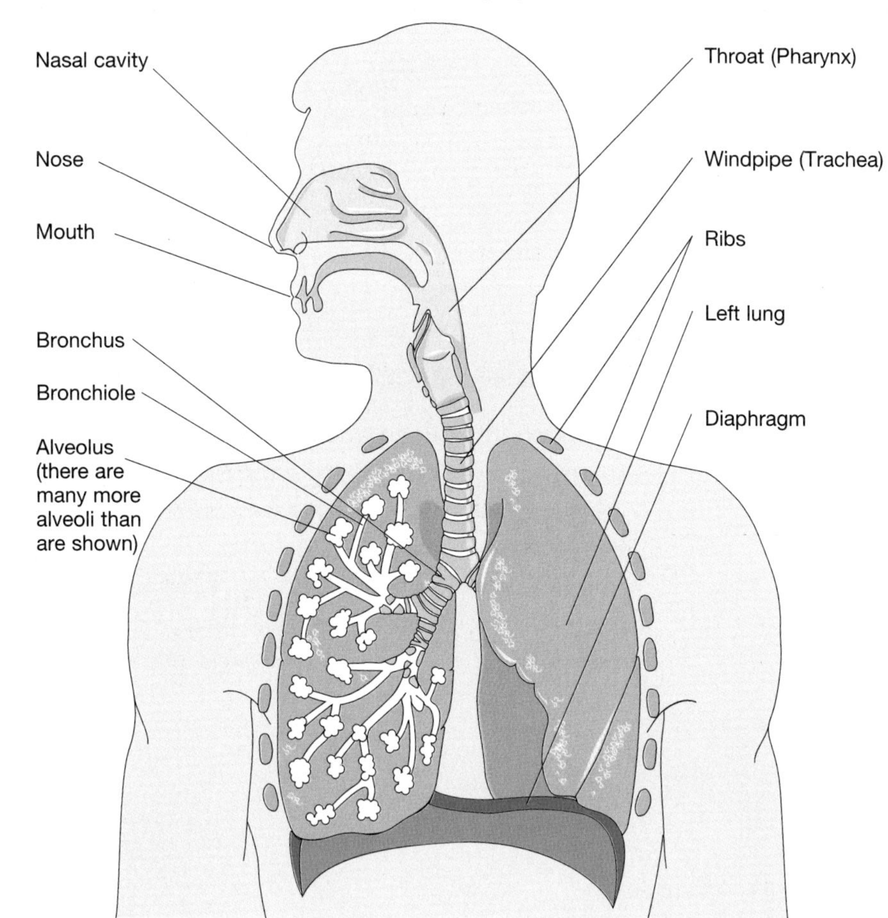

Note the position of the ribs.

Air enters the body through the respiratory tract. It passes through the mouth and nose, down the windpipe or **trachea** which divides into two bronchi – one into each lung. The bronchi subdivide into bronchioles and end in alveoli (see Table 1.9).

Table 1.9 Respiratory tract

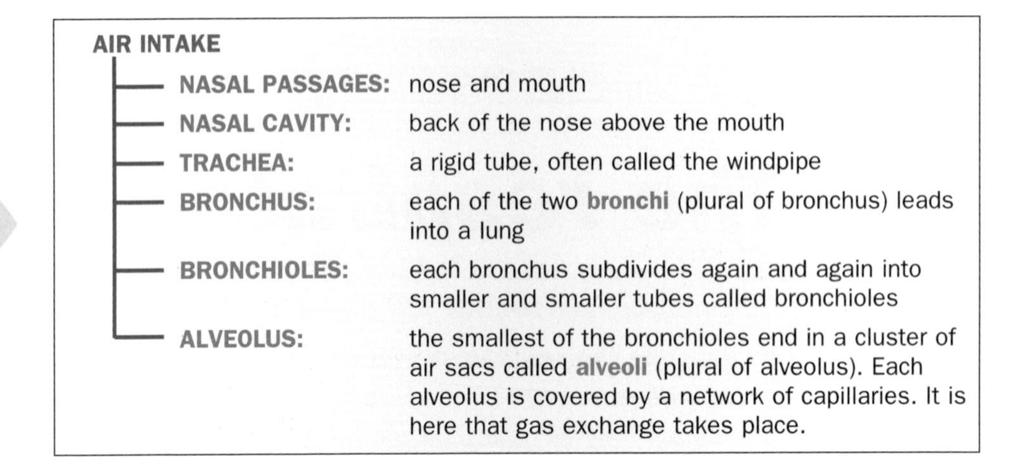

AIR INTAKE

NASAL PASSAGES:	nose and mouth
NASAL CAVITY:	back of the nose above the mouth
TRACHEA:	a rigid tube, often called the windpipe
BRONCHUS:	each of the two **bronchi** (plural of bronchus) leads into a lung
BRONCHIOLES:	each bronchus subdivides again and again into smaller and smaller tubes called bronchioles
ALVEOLUS:	the smallest of the bronchioles end in a cluster of air sacs called **alveoli** (plural of alveolus). Each alveolus is covered by a network of capillaries. It is here that gas exchange takes place.

You should be able to describe the respiratory tract.

Fig 1.17 The capillary network around the alveoli

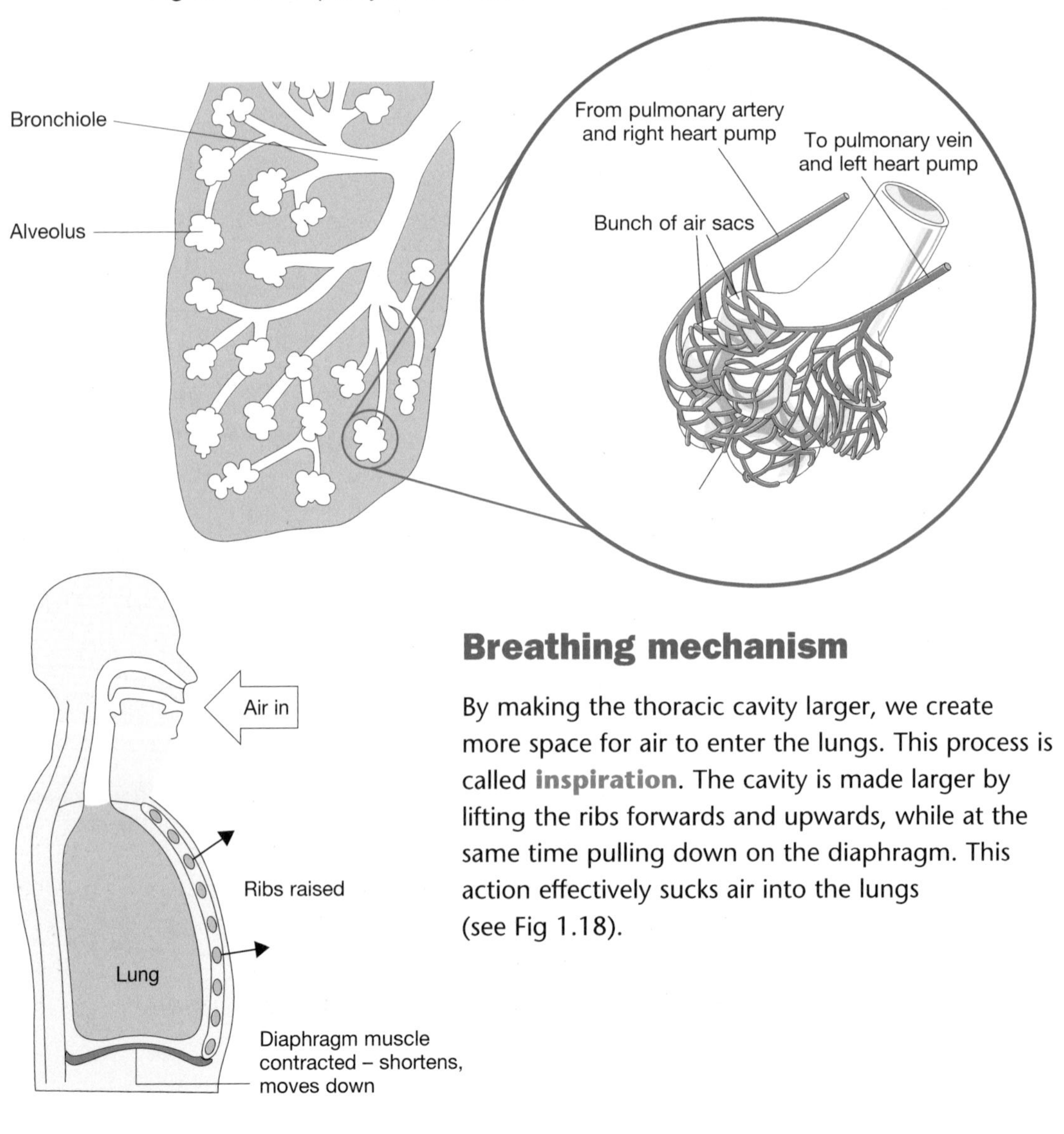

Fig 1.18 Inspiration - sucking air into the lungs

Breathing mechanism

By making the thoracic cavity larger, we create more space for air to enter the lungs. This process is called **inspiration**. The cavity is made larger by lifting the ribs forwards and upwards, while at the same time pulling down on the diaphragm. This action effectively sucks air into the lungs (see Fig 1.18).

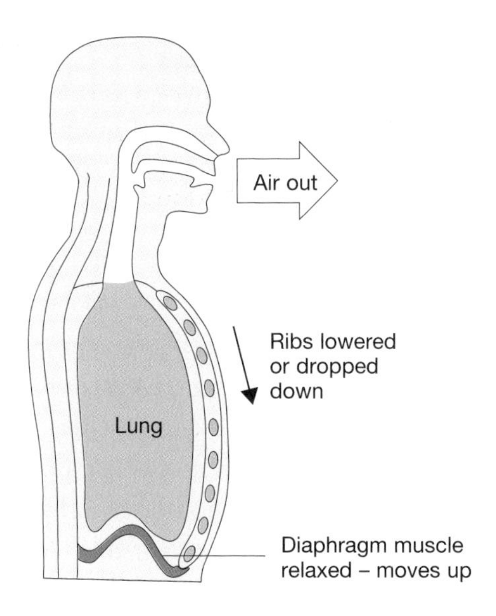

Breathing out, or exhaling, is the opposite of inspiration. The ribs are pulled down and back and the diaphragm is pulled up. This reduces the size of the thoracic cavity and effectively squeezes the air out. This is called **expiration** (see Fig 1.19).

Fig 1.19 Expiration – squeezing air out of the lungs

Lung capacities

We measure the amount of air that can be inspired using a machine called a **spirometer**. This draws a line on a moving sheet of paper to show the amount of air inspired and expired over a given period. This total lung capacity can be divided into sections (see Fig 1.20).

Note the four volumes and four capacities.

Fig 1.20 Spirometer trace

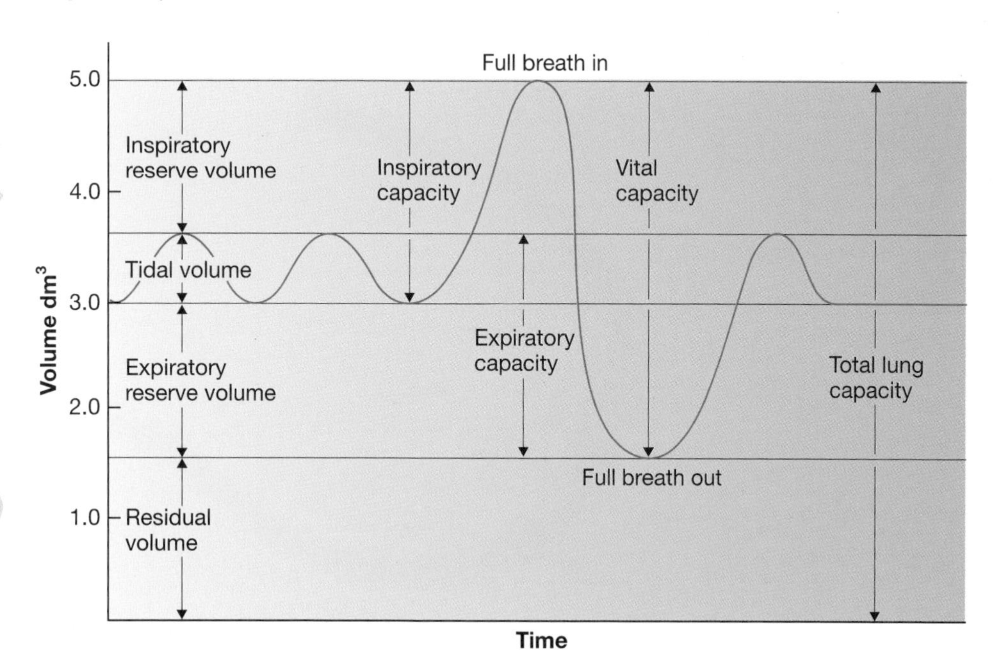

The values are given for a young healthy male. Those for an equivalent healthy young female would be around 20% lower.

Response to exercise

Exercise has a major effect on the lung capacity of an athlete. In the short term, breathing becomes more rapid during exercise and, at the same time, deeper. This means that more air is inspired during exercise and so more oxygen can be transferred to the blood stream. This is necessary to ensure that the muscles can work. This transfer of oxygen to the blood is called **gaseous exchange**.

Effects of exercise on the system

Although breathing becomes more rapid during exercise, the speed with which this occurs depends upon the amount of physical activity the individual is used to. Table 1.10 lists the major effects that training has on the respiratory system.

Table 1.10 Effects of training on the respiratory system

• The size of the chest increases
• The amount that the chest can expand increases
• The breathing rate at rest gets slower
• The capillary web around the alveolus is increased
• More alveoli are ready to pass gases to and from the blood
• The exchange of gas is improved
• Inspiratory and expiratory reserve volumes increase
• Tidal volume increases during exercise

After physical activity has taken place the sportsperson will continue to breathe deeply for some time. This is to remove any oxygen debt that may have developed (see Chapter 3). A well-trained, fitter person, however, will revert to normal breathing faster than an untrained person. This is due to their more efficient breathing mechanisms.

KEY POINT **If hard physical exercise is carried out quickly, then the muscles have to work without oxygen. This deficiency is called an oxygen debt.**

Oxygen and carbon dioxide exchange

AQA A | AQA B | EDEXCEL | OCR PE | OCR G | NICCEA

Fig 1.21 Detailed section of one air sac (alveolus) showing gas exchange

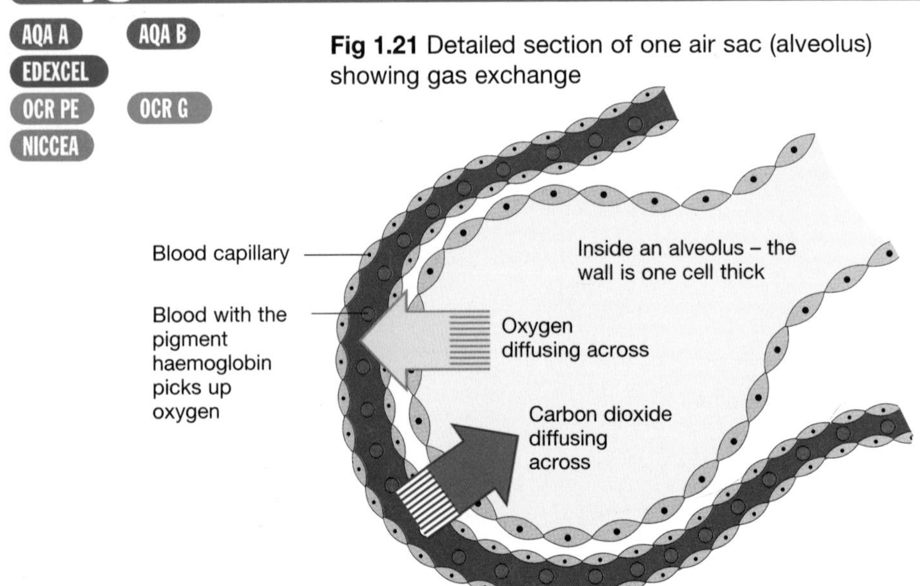

Not all oxygen is removed from the air when we breathe in at any one time. The amount of oxygen passed into the blood stream is called **oxygen uptake**. It depends on the type and intensity of the activity we are doing (see Table 1.11).

Table 1.11 Amount of O_2 and CO_2 present in inspired and expired air

	INSPIRED AIR	EXPIRED AT REST	EXPIRED DURING EXERCISE
O_2	21%	17%	15%
CO_2	0.03%	3%	6%

Oxygen uptake must not be confused with oxygen intake.

PROGRESS CHECK

1. Identify the major organs of the respiratory system.
2. What is vital capacity?
3. Explain the term oxygen uptake.

1. Nasal passages; windpipe; lungs. 2. Vital capacity is the combined total of the tidal volume, inspiratory reserve volume, and expiratory reserve volume. 3. Oxygen uptake is the term used to describe the amount of oxygen absorbed into the blood during each breath.

Sample GCSE questions

(a) Give the anatomical name for the following bones:

(i) kneecap *patella*

(ii) breastbone *sternum*

(iii) shin *tibia*

(iv) thigh bone *femur*

Make sure that you spell these terms correctly.

[4]

(b) **Flexion** and **extension** are two types of movement possible at a ball and socket joint. Give the **three** other movement possibilities

rotation/circumduction/adduction/abduction

Any three of these would be satisfactory.

[3]

(c) State which main muscle contracts for each of the following given actions:

(i) straightens the leg at the knee *quadriceps*

(ii) pulls your leg back at the hip *gluteals/gluteus maximus*

(iii) flexes your trunk so that you can bend forward *abdominals/hip flexors/ rectus abdominus*

You have a choice with the last two sections of this question: remember the spellings of these words.

[4]

(d) When the elbow flexes say which main muscle is the:

(i) antagonist *triceps*

(ii) agonist *biceps*

[2]

(e) Give a function for each of the following:

(i) red blood cells *carry oxygen*

(ii) white blood cells *fight bacteria/infection/disease*

(iii) platelets *clotting*

Simple answers are all that is called for.

[3]

(f) **(i)** State where in the lungs gas exchange takes place. *alveoli*

Give the anatomical name for windpipe. *trachea*

(ii) What happens to the diaphragm and ribs during expiration?

goes up/goes dome-shaped

move down and in

You must state the FULL movement of the ribs to get the mark.

[5]

EDEXCEL 1999 Paper 1 Q12, 14, 16, 19

Exam practice questions

1. **(a)** Give another name for the knee cap.

.... **[1]**

(b) Give **two** functions of the skeleton.

(i) ....

(ii) .... **[2]**

(c) Explain the following movements at a joint:

(i) flexion ....

(ii) extension ....

(iii) circumduction .... **[3]**

(d) Describe ligaments and their functions at synovial joints.

....

....

....

.... **[4]**

(e) Name the **three** types of muscle tissue found in the body and say where each may be found.

....

....

....

.... **[5]**

AQA 1996 QA1

Chapter

2 Fitness

The following topics are covered in this chapter:

- ***Definitions***
- ***Physical fitness***
- ***Components of physical fitness***
- ***Motor fitness***
- ***Improving fitness***

2.1 Definitions

After studying this section you should be able to:

- ***explain what fitness is and recall the major definitions of fitness***

What is fitness?

AQA A

WJEC

Be able to quote the definition given by your Board.

Fitness can mean different things to different people. The weightlifting champion has a different concept of fitness from that of the marathon runner. There are several definitions of fitness:

- the ability to perform physical tasks efficiently and effectively (NICCEA)
- the ability to meet the daily physical demands of work and play without excessive fatigue and still have something in reserve (AQA)
- a physical condition which is the result of differing fitness components working together to influence overall physical efficiency (WJEC)

What is common to all these definitions is the idea that physical fitness is the ability to perform **physical activity efficiently**, without placing **undue strain** on the body. When considering the idea of physical fitness we should always ask the question, **'fit for what?'**

Be able to distinguish between fitness, physical fitness and motor fitness.

When trying to answer this question we must take into account that fitness is divided into **two** main areas:

1. **physical fitness**
2. **motor fitness**

1. What two aspects are common to the major definitions of fitness discussed in this topic?
2. What two areas is fitness divided into?

1. The ability to perform physical activity efficiently without undue stress. 2. Physical fitness and motor fitness.

2.2 Physical fitness

LEARNING SUMMARY

After studying this section you should be able to:

- ***explain physical fitness and describe the effects that physical activity has on the body systems***

What is physical fitness?

AQA A | AQA B | EDEXCEL | OCR PE | OCR G | WJEC | NICCEA

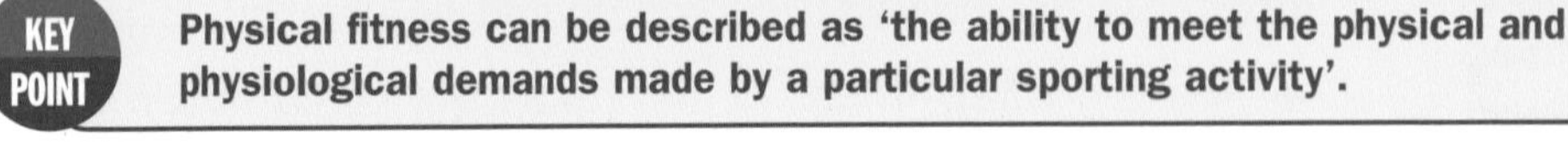
KEY POINT

Physical fitness can be described as 'the ability to meet the physical and physiological demands made by a particular sporting activity'.

How does physical activity affect us?

Participation in physical activity alters the ways in which various body systems work (see Table 2.1).

Table 2.1 Changes observed in some of the body's systems brought on by physical activity

Be aware of these significant changes.

	AT REST	DURING ACTIVITY
Depth of breathing	8 litres/minute	25 litres/minute
Pulse rate	75 beats/minute	190+ beats/minute
Stroke volume	100 ml/beat	200 ml/beat
Cardiac output*	7 litres/minute	35+ litres/minute
O_2 used per min	250 ml/minute	4500+ ml/minute
Size of O_2 debt developed	none	10+ litres

*__Cardiac output__ is the volume of blood pumped by the left ventricle of the heart in 1 minute. It is measured in litres/minute. The sign for cardiac output is **Q**.

The ability of the body to cope with these changes depends on how prepared it is for the demands that are being placed on it.

KEY POINT

The body adjusts to the demands that are made on it regularly.

Someone who runs a little further each day will find that it gets gradually easier to run for longer as their respiratory system becomes more efficient. When someone's body systems can meet the demands of exercise without undue stress, they are said to be in a **normal state**. However, the normal state will change as more and more regular physical demands are made. The body is able to adjust to regular participation in physical activity.

PROGRESS CHECK

1. How can physical fitness be described?
2. What happens to the body when regular demands are made on it?
3. What does Q stand for?

1. The ability to meet the physical and psychological demands made by a particular sporting activity. 2. It adjusts to these demands. 3. Cardiac output (the amount of blood pumped out by the left ventricle in 1 minute).

2.3 Components of physical fitness

After studying this section you should be able to:

- *identify and describe the four major components of physical fitness*

Strength, stamina, speed and suppleness

AQA A AQA B EDEXCEL OCR PE OCR G WJEC NICCEA

Physical fitness can be said to have **four** major components: **strength**, **stamina**, **speed** and **suppleness**. These are often referred to as the **4 Ss** (see Fig 2.1).

Be able to describe the 4 Ss.

Fig 2.1 The four main components of physical fitness

STRENGTH — PHYSICAL FITNESS — STAMINA

SUPPLENESS* — PHYSICAL FITNESS — SPEED

*Suppleness is often referred to as flexibility

The balance of each of these components required by a player varies according to the demands of each particular sport.

Strength

KEY POINT

Strength is defined as 'the ability to use muscles to apply force to overcome resistance'.

There are **three** types of strength, each being suited to a different physical activity (see Table 2.2):

Know and be able to differentiate between these.

1. **static** strength
2. **explosive** strength
3. **dynamic** strength

Table 2.2 Analysis of strength types

	STATIC	EXPLOSIVE	DYNAMIC
Activity example	tug of war rugby scrum	shot put high jump	rowing 100 m sprint
Body state	stays the same	moves fast	moves fast
Distance moved	little or none	little	can be considerable
Time taken	varies, but not long	small amount	can be considerable
Muscle state	stays the same	changes quickly	changes quickly and repeatedly

Photo 2.1 An example of static strength combined with balance

Speed

Speed is defined as 'the shortest time taken to move the body or a body part over a specific distance'.

The ability to move all or part of the body quickly is essential in many sporting activities. Speed may be assisted by many different body parts, e.g. the legs in running, the arms in swimming and gymnastics. In some sports, only one part of the body moves fast: in fencing it is the rapid straightening of the arm that can win a point; in karate it might be the fast movement of the foot that wins a point. In other sports, such as archery, speed is not demanded in competition – accuracy is all important.

Stamina

Stamina is defined as 'the ability to perform strenuous activity over a long period of time'.

Stamina is often referred to as **cardiovascular fitness**. In order to meet the requirements of cardiovascular fitness, there must be a continuous supply of O_2 (oxygen) to the muscles, so that energy can be produced. This is achieved through the blood supply, which also removes waste matter (see Chapter 3).

The term 'cardiovascular' relates to:
cardio – heart
vascular – blood vessels

If the body is worked hard over a long period of time, then an **oxygen debt** will develop (see page 37). This eventually results in the build-up of **lactic acid** in the muscles, which in turn brings on a feeling of fatigue and can lead to **cramp** in some muscles. Many sports demand stamina, especially those such as rowing and long-distance running.

Suppleness

Suppleness is defined as 'the range of movement possible at a joint or joints'.

Suppleness is often referred to as **flexibility** or **mobility**. Suppleness is affected by the type of joint and the muscle attachments to it. Some joints, such as the hip, move freely giving a wide range of movement (see Photo 2.2).

Photo 2.2 This activity shows a wide range of movement at the hip

Others joints, such as those between the vertebrae, have a very limited range of movement. They overcome this deficiency by working together to give a more extensive range of movement.

Be able to identify a sporting activity to illustrate each physical fitness component.

Training can increase the suppleness of all types of joints. A greater range of movement at a joint may be of advantage in some sports, e.g. the butterfly swimmer needs to have a wide range of movement in the shoulders. However, the weightlifter places greater emphasis on strength and requires only a limited range of movement at the shoulder.

Table 2.3 Physical fitness components of some sporting activities

	STRENGTH	STAMINA	SPEED	SUPPLENESS
Rowing	yes	yes	some	some
Aerobics	some	yes	yes	yes
Skating	some	some	some	some
Soccer	some	yes	some	some
Archery	some	little	little	little

PROGRESS CHECK

1. List three types of strength.
2. Which type of strength is rowing an example of?
3. What does the build up of lactic acid cause?

1. Static, dynamic, explosive. 2. Dynamic. 3. Fatigue and cramp in the muscles.

2.4 Motor fitness

LEARNING SUMMARY

After studying this section you should be able to:

- *define motor fitness, and describe the main components*

What is motor fitness?

AQA A AQA B EDEXCEL OCR PE OCR G WJEC NICCEA

KEY POINT

Motor fitness can be defined as 'the ability to perform successfully in a given sporting context'.

These are often referred to as the skill-related aspects of fitness.

To achieve success in any sporting context, all components of physical fitness are needed. However, motor fitness directly affects the sportsperson's ability to perform the skills needed in their chosen physical activity.

The main components of motor fitness are listed below.

- **Power** – the combination of strength and speed working together.
- **Agility** – the ability to change body position and direction quickly and with precision.
- **Co-ordination** – the ability to perform complex motor tasks involving several skills in sequence, as in hurdling.
- **Balance** – an awareness of the body's position in a fast-changing physical situation, such as in gymnastic activity on the beam.
- **Reaction** – the time taken to respond to a given stimulus.
- **Attitude** – the psychological approach applied by the sportsperson to the sporting situation, often described as the 'will to win' factor. This element of motor fitness is often overlooked.

Be able to describe each of the main components of motor fitness.

Fig 2.2 Major components of motor fitness

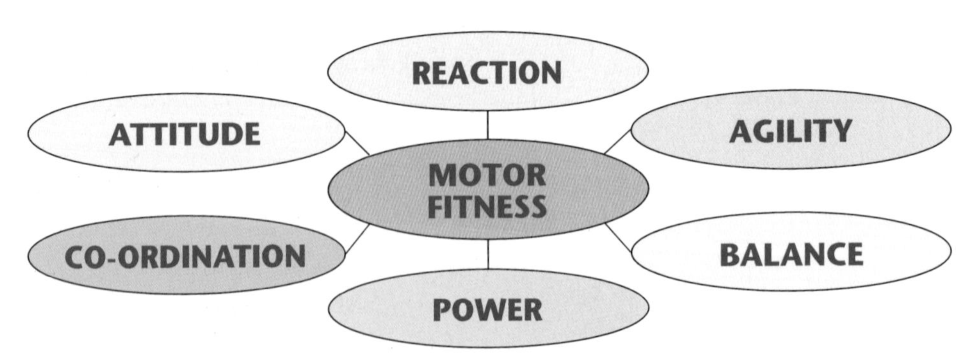

PROGRESS CHECK

1. Define motor fitness.
2. List four components of motor fitness and describe them.
3. Give another name for the components of motor fitness.

1. The ability to perform successfully in a sporting context. 2. Selection of any of the six listed earlier, described correctly. 3. They are often called skill-related aspects.

2.5 Improving fitness

After studying this section you should be able to:

- ***describe the four guiding principles related to fitness improvement***
- ***describe the FITT principles relating to fitness improvement***

Fitness principles

AQA B

OCR PE

The four principles

The physical fitness of the human body can always be improved. This can be done by following a relevant training programme. Some programmes are more effective than others.

There are **four guiding principles** which can help sportspeople to decide on an effective programme. They are:

You must be able to quote these four principles.

1. **overload**
2. **progression**
3. **specificity**
4. **reversibility**

Overload

This is the term used to describe activities that impose demands on the body which are greater than usual. The overload principal aims to put the body systems under repeated stress. If excessive repeated demand is put on a muscle, then more fibres will be prepared for work; if excessive demand is placed on the body's aerobic system, it will produce more red blood cells – more oxygen can be taken up and it is used more effectively.

It is possible to increase **aerobic activity**, **muscular strength** and **flexibility** by using the overload principle.

Overload can be attained in three ways.

1. Increasing the **intensity** of the activity – this might mean that we have to run faster, lift heavier weights or stretch further during training. This builds up over a period of time.
2. Increasing the **frequency** of the activity – this means that there should be more training sessions with shorter rest periods between them.
3. Increasing the **duration** of the activity – this means that the length of each training session should be increased progressively.

If all three methods of overload were to be used at one time, then training sessions would be harder work, more frequent and would take longer.

Progression

Remember that progression should be gradual.

A training session should always be within the capabilities of the individual. Although stress must be placed on the body systems for the training to be effective, too much stress too soon can cause injury.

If the overload of the body systems is increased at a steady and attainable rate, then improvements can be monitored easily and progression noted. However, it must be remembered that the body adapts and will begin to find the harder programmes less demanding as time goes by. Thus, the overload must be increased, otherwise progression will stop.

Specificity

Training should be specific. This means that it should concentrate on the particular needs of the performer. Lifting weights, for example, will increase muscle strength, but it will have little effect upon aerobic capacity.

Be able to quote exercises for specific body parts.

Not only should the training be specific to the particular sport, but it should also be specific to those parts of the body that contribute most to the sport. If upper body strength is required, then exercise concentrating on the arms and chest will be needed. If both speed and endurance are required, then exercises should be devised with this in mind.

A specific programme could be designed for a person returning from injury. If the muscles of one leg are recovering from a strain or pull, they cannot be worked as hard as those of the leg that has not been damaged. Lower levels of stress should be put on recently repaired body tissue. However, by carefully designing a programme which is specific to the recovering part of the body, effective rehabilitation should result.

Reversibility

It is estimated that strength is lost three times more quickly than it is gained.

Just as the body adapts to greater stress, so it will adapt to less stress being placed on it. If training stops for a period of time, fitness will be impaired. It should be noted that the body adapts to lower stress levels far more quickly than it does to high stress levels.

Anaerobic activities are affected less than aerobic ones as they do not need vast amounts of oxygen. The aerobic capacity of muscle deteriorates very quickly. If the muscles are not used, they begin to **atrophy**: this means that they waste away and become smaller and thinner. Weaker muscles are more prone to injury.

The FITT principles

AQA A | AQA B | EDEXCEL | OCR PE | OCR G | WJEC | NICCEA

When referring to principles of training many people like to use the mnemonic 'FITT'. This is a slightly different way of remembering the principles described above. **FITT** stands for:

- **F – frequency** (how often you should exercise)
- **I – intensity** (how hard you should exercise)
- **T – time** (how long you should exercise for)
- **T – type** (what exercises you consider suitable for your chosen sport)

These also relate to overload, progression and specificity, but overlook reversibility.

PROGRESS CHECK

1. List the three ways in which overload can be attained.
2. Explain how duration can be used to increase overload.
3. When might muscle atrophy occur? Explain this term.

1. Intensity, frequency, duration. 2. The length of each training session can be increased.
3. When training stops, muscles might atrophy, i.e. get smaller and thinner.

Sample GCSE questions

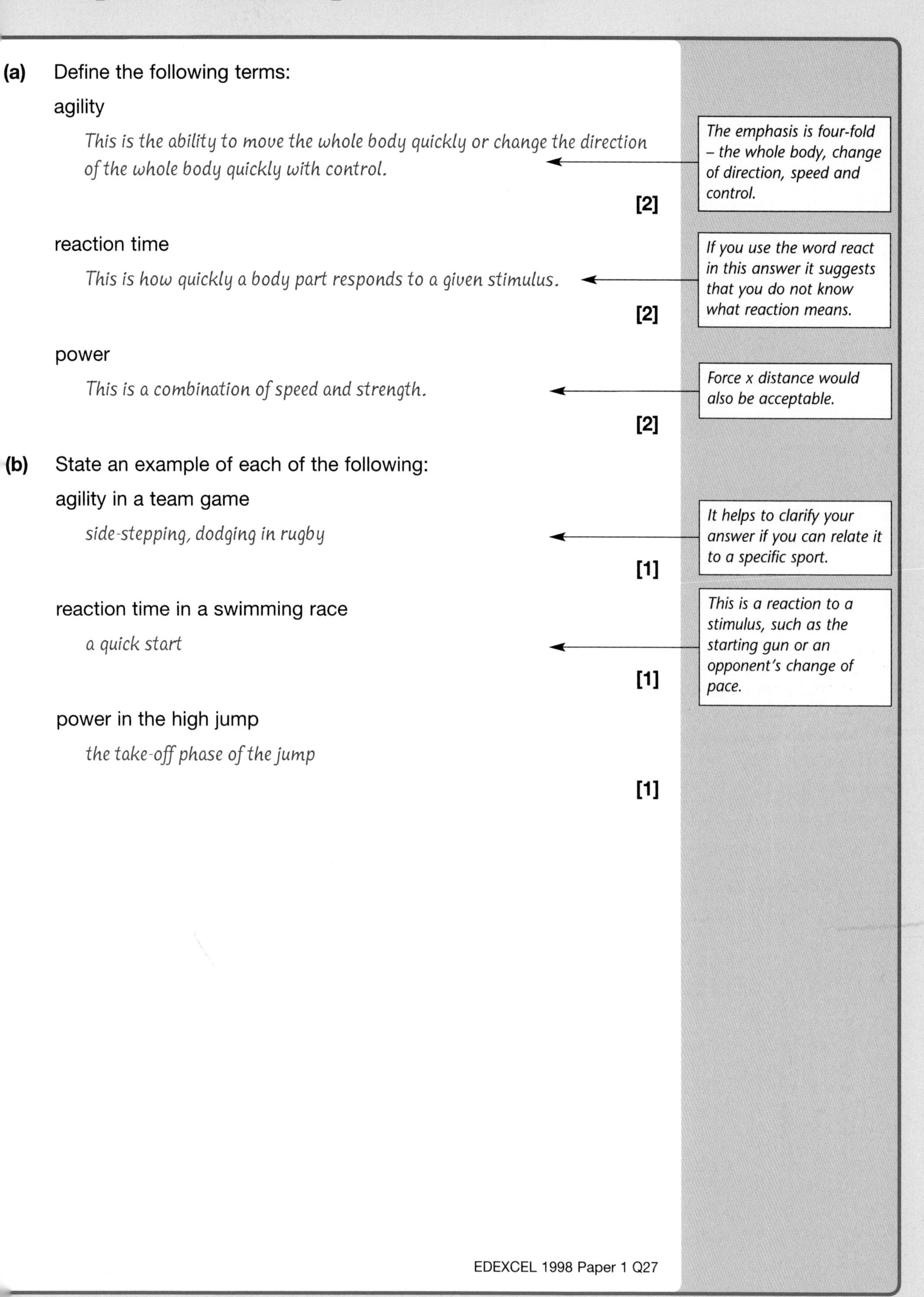

(a) Define the following terms:

agility

This is the ability to move the whole body quickly or change the direction of the whole body quickly with control.

[2]

> *The emphasis is four-fold – the whole body, change of direction, speed and control.*

reaction time

This is how quickly a body part responds to a given stimulus.

[2]

> *If you use the word react in this answer it suggests that you do not know what reaction means.*

power

This is a combination of speed and strength.

[2]

> *Force x distance would also be acceptable.*

(b) State an example of each of the following:

agility in a team game

side-stepping, dodging in rugby

[1]

> *It helps to clarify your answer if you can relate it to a specific sport.*

reaction time in a swimming race

a quick start

[1]

> *This is a reaction to a stimulus, such as the starting gun or an opponent's change of pace.*

power in the high jump

the take-off phase of the jump

[1]

EDEXCEL 1998 Paper 1 Q27

Exam practice questions

Mohammed is an 'up-and-coming' badminton player and is told that his standard of play will improve if he increases his level of fitness. He starts training three times a week, for an hour each session.

Week number	Session 1	Session 2	Session 3
1	running session	speed work on court with shuttle	weights session

(a) State which aspect of the FITT principles relates to each of the following:

(i) an hour each session ....

(ii) three times a week..

(ii) speed work on court with a shuttle.. **[3]**

There are several other principles of training in addition to the FITT principles. Answer the following questions relating to these other principles.

(b) Which principle of training should be applied to the programme to ensure that Mohammed's fitness continues to improve?

.... **[1]**

(c) Which principle of training should be applied to the programme to reduce the chance of injury?

.... **[1]**

(d) Which principle of training will apply if he stops training for a couple of months?

.... **[1]**

(e) Which principle of training needs to be considered if he takes up basketball instead of badminton and wants a fitness programme for this activity instead?

.... **[1]**

EDEXCEL 1999 Paper 1 Q29

Chapter 3 Training methods and programmes

The following topics are covered in this chapter:

- *Training threshold*
- *Oxygen debt*
- *Training methods*
- *Training programmes*

3.1 Training threshold

After studying this section you should be able to:

- ***explain what a training threshold is***
- ***establish maximum heart rate and work out a training threshold***

What is a training threshold?

AQA A AQA B EDEXCEL OCR PE OCR G WJEC NICCEA

As we have seen, training can be effective only if the body's systems are put under stress (see page 31). So, there must be a suitable element of **overload** in any training programme. This means that we have to be able to establish the **safe yet effective** level that an individual should train at. This is known as the **training threshold**. Physical work done below this level will have little or no effect on the improvement of fitness. However, work done too far above this level can lead to injury.

A training threshold rate is a safe and effective level to work at.

Working out a maximum heart rate and a related training threshold

AQA A AQA B EDEXCEL OCR PE OCR G WJEC NICCEA

Maximum heart rate

To be able to calculate your correct training threshold, it is important to establish your **maximum heart rate** in beats per minute. Many people use the accepted formula that your maximum heart rate should always be **220 beats per minute minus your age**. Some suggest **180** as the maximum and yet others claim that the maximum level **varies with age**.

These are all rather crude – but essentially safe ways of establishing a maximum heart rate – as they take into account that the maximum declines as a person gets older. This has been shown by scientific research.

Be aware of the different methods.

A more exact and scientific way of establishing your maximum heart rate is to undertake a test on, for example, a treadmill. This means that a person has to work at maximal effort for a given period of time (see Photo 3.1).

Photo 3.1 Treadmill work

Using the maximum heart rate to calculate a training threshold

However the maximum heart rate is established, it can be used to determine the appropriate **training threshold rate** (**TTR**) for an individual. There are a number of ways that this can be done and each is effective in its own way.

- **The 180 method** – deduct your age from 180. This method assumes that your maximum heart rate is 180. Thus the safe and effective training threshold for a 40-year-old person would be 180 – 40 = 140.
- **The 70% to 80% method** – this is based on a person working at 70% to 80% of a **notional** maximum heart rate that is related to a given age (see Table 3.1).

Notional is not the same as maximal.

Table 3.1 Table used to calculate training thresholds

Age	Maximum heart rate (beats per minute)	Safe working rate (beats per minute)
20	200	140/160
30	190	133/152
40	180	126/144
50	170	119/136

The 180 method and the 70% to 80% method presuppose a maximum heart rate.

- **The 60% method** – this calculates the threshold level by adding 60% of the range of your heart rate to the resting pulse rate.

  For example:
  if a person's resting pulse rate = 80
  and his maximum rate = 180
  then the range = (180 - 80) = 100
  60% of the range = 60
  so the threshold rate = (80 + 60) = 140
- **Karvonen's formula** – this method establishes the threshold as follows:
  establish resting rate = 60
  establish maximum rate = 200
  then the range = (200 - 60) = 140
  70% of the range = 98
  so threshold rate = (98 + 60) = 158

You should be able to work out a threshold rate for a given set of figures.

To use the 60% method or Karvonen's formula a person must be able to establish his own maximum heart rate correctly.

The 60% method is more suitable for strength work, while Karvonen's formula is more suitable for aerobic training.

1. What two factors does the training threshold rate refer to?
2. Which method of calculating the TTR is most appropriate to strength training?

1. The safe level for training; the effective level for training. 2. 60% method.

3.2 Oxygen debt

After studying this section you should be able to:

- ***describe how ATP supplies muscles with energy***
- ***understand the terms aerobic and anaerobic***

How ATP supplies muscles with energy

AQA A AQA B EDEXCEL OCR PE OCR G WJEC NICCEA

Training requires a great deal of muscular exertion. This means that throughout exercise the muscles are continually contracting and relaxing. This muscular exertion requires **energy**. Energy comes from a substance called **adenosine triphosphate** (**ATP**) which, during exercise, breaks down to a second substance called **adenosine diphosphate** (**ADP**) and this produces energy. The energy that is stored in ATP comes from the reaction between glucose and oxygen (see page 81).

ATP is stored in muscle fibres but is used up quickly.

Aerobic and anaerobic activity

AQA A AQA B EDEXCEL OCR PE OCR G WJEC NICCEA

aerobic = with oxygen
anaerobic = without oxygen.

Aerobic activity

If a lot of oxygen is present, then energy production is carried out **aerobically**. As this type of physical activity requires large amounts of oxygen, the level of work must be of low intensity, but it may continue for a long period of time. Long distance running is an aerobic activity.

Anaerobic activity

If there is a shortage of oxygen, then energy production is carried out **anaerobically**. This type of physical work is usually of high intensity, lasts for a short period of time, requires a great deal of energy, but happens so fast that there is not enough time to get lots of oxygen to the muscles. The 100 m sprint is an anaerobic activity.

If anaerobic activity takes place over a long period of time, the muscles soon become exhausted. This is due to a condition called **oxygen debt**.

Be able to describe this process.

Strenuous exercise uses up all ATP stores and causes a build-up of **lactic acid**. This is a **toxic** (poisonous) substance which causes the muscles to stop working. Lactic acid can only be removed in the presence of oxygen and upon completion of hard strenuous exercise it is essential that the oxygen debt is repaid. Large amounts of oxygen are needed for this **oxygen recovery**. This is why we pant after hard exercise. In this way ATP stores are replenished and lactic acid removed from the muscular system (see Fig 3.1).

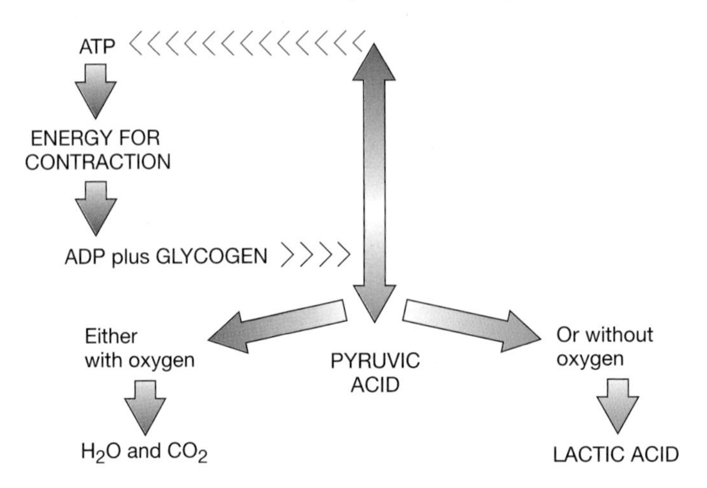

Fig 3.1 Lactic acid energy system

By establishing a suitable training threshold rate it should be possible to train effectively, while at the same time avoiding the build-up of lactic acid which could bring training to a premature end.

1. Which substance do we get energy from?
2. What is the major difference between aerobic and anaerobic activity?
3. What substance builds up in the muscles during prolonged anaerobic activity?

1. ATP; adenosine triphosphate. 2. Aerobic activity uses oxygen at the time of exercise; anaerobic activity does not use oxygen at the time. 3. Lactic acid.

3.3 Training methods

After studying this section you should be able to:

- ***describe a number of different training methods***
- ***describe the advantages of each method***

What are some different training methods?

AQA A, AQA B, EDEXCEL, OCR PE, OCR G, WJEC, NICCEA

There is a wide range of different training methods and all are, to some extent, effective. All place an emphasis on a number of the fitness components described earlier (see page 27).

Interval training

Rest periods allow for recovery from oxygen debt.

This involves alternating periods of high intensity work with rest periods. During rest periods the sportsperson may be inactive - their body stops moving – or they may work at a low intensity.

Examples of interval training are:
- swimming 10 x 50 m sprints with a 20 second rest between each leg
- running 10 x 100 m sprints with a 300 m jog between each sprint

With this type of training there are four ways in which the stress level can be increased. These are to:

These are examples of overload.

- increase the speed of the sprint
- increase the number of sprints
- increase the distance sprinted
- decrease the rest periods

The advantage of interval training is that it is easy to measure progress and improvement.

Continuous training

This is at the training threshold rate.

This form of training is often called **LSD** (**Long Slow Distance**). It involves working for a prolonged period of time at a steady stress level. The intensity of the work is just below the point at which an **oxygen debt** would develop. At the start of the programme, an individual may work for only 20 or 30 minutes. However, over a number of sessions, the time spent would increase, although the workload would probably remain the same.

KEY POINT **The LSD method is suitable for long-distance swimmers, runners and cyclists as it develops stamina rather than speed.**

The advantages of continuous training are that it:
- requires very little equipment
- is good for aerobic fitness
- is often easy to do

Fartlek training

The oxygen debt is replaced during low-level work.

This form of training takes its name from a type of programme developed in Scandinavia. The word means '**speed play**', and this describes the way the method works. Fartlek is very similar to continuous training but also includes short, sharp bursts of effort at a much higher intensity. These may be of only 5 or 10 seconds' duration but could occur every 2 or 3 minutes. If the high level of work lasts for longer than this, then it is repeated less frequently.

The advantages of Fartlek training are that it:
- can be adapted easily to suit the individual
- reflects the pattern of games that have a regular change of pace, e.g. football, hockey

Circuit training

The order of events is important.

This type of work includes a number of physical activities performed one after the other in the form of a circle or circuit. There are two basic variations: fixed load and individual load. Both follow a similar pattern.

1. **Fixed load** – the individual attempts to perform each exercise continually over a given time. When this is achieved, the circuit is redesigned to increase the stress level by setting a new target (e.g. lengthening the work periods or shortening the rest periods).
2. **Individual load** – the individual establishes **their own** level of work for each exercise. This is usually between 50% and 60% of the maximum that a person can do for 1 minute of the exercise. They are then timed for each circuit of exercises and aim to be faster each time they do the circuit. With individual load circuits it is possible to increase stress by reducing the rest periods between the exercises and by increasing the load level.

Circuits can be designed to build up strength, increase local muscular endurance or improve total stamina. Fig 3.2 shows an example of a simple six-station circuit. Note that each exercise puts stress on a different part of the body and that each body part is worked in turn.

Fig 3.2 A simple six-station circuit

You could be asked to write out a circuit.

STEP-UPS (legs) → PRESS-UPS (arms)

↓

SHUTTLE RUN (legs)

↓

SIT-UPS (stomach) → SKIPPING (legs)

↑

ARM CURLS (arms)

↑ (back to STEP-UPS)

KEY: The main parts of the body being overloaded are written in brackets.
This type of circuit will help to improve both strength and stamina.

Photo 3.2 Sit-ups

Photo 3.3 Press-ups

The advantages of circuit training are that:

- the variety of exercises prevents boredom
- as exercises can be done inside, there is no need to worry about the weather
- any kind of exercise can be included
- it is easy to measure progress

Weight training

Weight training can be very similar to circuit training. The individual completes a set of exercises in a prescribed order using weights, rather than doing a range of different activities. Each station concentrates on a different part of the body.

The number of times that a weight is lifted is called repetitions or reps.

As training progresses, the weights can be made heavier and rest periods can be reduced. As a general rule, it is agreed that in order to increase strength a person should lift heavy weights but with few reps. To increase stamina a light weight should be lifted but with a large number of reps. An example of a weights circuit is shown in Fig 3.3.

Fig 3.3 Example of a weight training programme (diagrams of the exercises are shown in Fig 3.4)

EXERCISE	MAIN MUSCLE GROUPS UNDER STRESS
Bench press	chest, front of shoulder, back of upper arm
Front squat	thigh, hip
Two hands curl	front of upper arm
Deep knee bend	legs, back, chest
Side to side bend	sides of trunk, stomach
Heel lift	lower leg, ankle

EACH EXERCISE TO BE COMPLETED FIVE TIMES
EACH SET OF EXERCISES TO BE COMPLETED TWICE.

To increase **INTENSITY** the size of the weights used in each activity would be increased.
To increase **DURATION** the number of sets of exercises would be increased.
To increase **FREQUENCY** the number of sessions would be increased.

In this type of activity the individual should start with easily manageable weights and progress to heavier weights gradually.

Fig 3.4 Weight training exercises

There are **two** main variations of weight training.

Be able to explain the difference between isometric and isotonic contractions.

1. **Isometric** weight training – this involves lifting the weight and hol muscular contraction for up to 5 seconds, then relaxing before repeating th exercise. This means that the overload of the muscle takes place when the contracted muscle fibres **are still**. They remain at the contracted length; they do not move. This type of contraction develops strength rather than endurance.
2. **Isotonic** weight training – this involves raising and lowering the weights repeatedly and rapidly. This means that muscle overload is taking place as the muscle fibres **move**: they are continually shortening and lengthening. This type of contraction develops stamina as well as strength.

The advantages of weight training are that it can be:

- a fast way to build up strength
- adapted to suit most sports
- carried out easily on multi-station weight machines

Table 3.2 Fitness components most affected by different training methods

	INTERVAL	CONTINUOUS	FARTLEK	CIRCUIT	WEIGHT
Strength				✓	✓
Speed	✓		✓		
Stamina		✓	✓	✓	✓
Suppleness	✓				
Power	✓				
Agility				✓	✓
Aerobic capacity		✓	✓	✓	
Anaerobic capacity	✓		✓	✓	✓

Pressure training

This type of training is often related to a particular skill, such as passing or heading in football. Once a person has learned the skill of heading, the skill should be practiced in a pressure situation. The player now has to head a number of balls which are delivered in turn at a fairly rapid pace. The player has to adjust to each heading situation quickly. If the balls are fed too quickly or the player becomes fatigued, the skill might well break down. A drill for pressure heading is shown in Fig 3.5.

Fig 3.5 Pressure heading drill

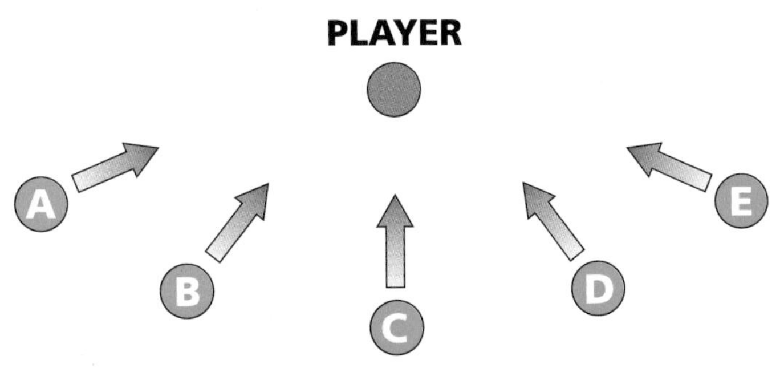

BALLS FED IN TURN TO PLAYER. SPEED OF FEED IS GRADUALLY INCREASED.

The advantage of pressure training is that it demonstrates a person's ability to perform specific skills in a stress situation.

Flexibility training

The body's flexibility can be improved by carrying out a series of mobility exercises for the joints. Each joint should be exercised in turn and can be stretched or moved to just beyond its **point of resistance**. For improvement to take place, the stretch should be held for 8 to 10 seconds, and the mobility exercises should be carried out for at least 10 minutes. To be fully effective the mobility exercises should be carried out approximately three times per week.

Photo 3.4 Active static stretching

Photo 3.5 Active static stretching

Photo 3.6 Passive static stretching

There are **two** main types of flexibility exercises.

1. **Static stretching**: this is moving the joint to beyond its point of resistance and holding the position still for 8 to 10 seconds. This can be done in either a **passive** or **active** manner. Passive stretching is when a partner forces the performer to stretch the joint (see Photo 3.6); active stretching is when the performer forces the joint on his own (see Photos 3.4 and 3.5).
2. **Ballistic stretching**: this uses momentum to move a body part at the joint. Exercises such as arm swinging, bouncing, twisting and turning are ballistic moves (see Fig 3.6).

Take great care with ballistic exercises. They should be attempted only by those with a good degree of flexibility.

Fig 3.6 Ballistic stretching

The advantages of flexibility training are that:

- it is cheap and easy to do
- little equipment is needed
- exercises can be done alone
- not a lot of space is needed

PROGRESS CHECK

1. Explain the term 'Fartlek'.
2. Explain how weight-training exercises should be performed to increase strength.
3. Explain the difference between active and passive stretches.
4. Explain the difference between isometric and isotonic contractions.

1. 'Speed play', e.g. running with a repeated change of pace. 2. To increase strength use heavy weights with a low number of reps. 3. Passive stretch is done with a partner; active is done alone. 4. In an isometric contraction the muscle fibres stay the same length and the load is held still; in isotonic contraction the load is moved and the fibres continually contract and relax.

3.4 Training programmes

After studying this section you should be able to:

- *describe the different parts of a session and know the value of rest periods*
- *describe the short and long-term effects of training*
- *describe a training programme*

Parts of a training session

AQA A AQA B EDEXCEL OCR PE OCR G WJEC NICCEA

Keep to the order shown here.

Training sessions must be structured. They must include:

1. a warm-up
2. the training activity
3. a cool down
4. rest period

The warm-up

A **warm-up** is essential – you should never attempt a training session without a warm-up. It should include a number of exercises that will gradually get the whole body ready for work. The exercises must:

Be able to construct a warm-up session.

- raise the blood flow to the muscles (i.e. increase your pulse rate)
- include stretching exercises to prepare the joints and muscles for harder work to come
- raise the body temperature
- prepare the mind for the physical work ahead

The warm-up is essential if injury is to be avoided during training.

The training activity

The **training activity** can take many forms, but it should be interesting as well as useful. The exercises should be varied and relate to the sport that you are training for. Prolonged work on a small number of exercises can become boring and the effects of the training will be reduced. When choosing exercises it is important to remember the principles of overload, progression, specificity and reversibility described in Chapter 2 (see page 31).

The cool down

Be able to explain the value of the cool down.

The **cool down** is important as it helps your body to return to normal. When a hard physical training session ends, an increased supply of blood is maintained in the muscles. This is because it is important to get rid of any oxygen debt that might have developed. However, the blood should be returned to general circulation as soon as possible to avoid **pooling**. If pooling occurs it can contribute to a feeling of faintness and dizziness. The type of exercises to be included should be similar to those in the warm-up, but should gradually decrease in intensity.

Rest periods

Rest periods are as important to training as hard physical exercise. During intensive and repeated periods of physical work, muscle fibres may become slightly damaged and develop a shortage of glycogen. The inclusion of rest days, when only light training or no physical work is done, allows the muscles to recover naturally.

Rest days or light training days are most important just before competition. They allow the sportsperson to enter the competition with their body fully prepared.

Short and long-term effects of training

AQA A AQA B EDEXCEL OCR PE OCR G WJEC NICCEA

Be able to differentiate between long and short-term effects of training.

For training to be effective, it must continue over a long period of time. However, training exercises also have immediate short-term effects (see Table 3.3).

Table 3.3 Short-term effects of exercise

Effect	Reason
increased rate of breathing (panting)	more oxygen needed for muscles to work, helps body stay cool
rise in pulse rate	transports more oxygen to muscles and removes waste materials, i.e. CO_2
sweating	helps body to stay cool
go red	blood moves to just below skin surface to radiate heat outwards and help to keep the body cool
blood diverted to muscles from other organs	diverted to muscles that are working hard
rise in body temperature	this is a by-product produced as muscles work hard

Prolonged training has a number of effects on various body parts (see Table 3.4).

Table 3.4 Long-term effects of training on various body parts

Body part	Effect
heart	• resting rate gets slower • range increases • increases slightly in size • **stroke volume** (blood forced out by each beat of the heart) increases
lungs	• maximal inspiratory and expiratory levels increase • more alveoli are ready for work • increase in capillary beds in alveoli
chest	• increase in size • ability to expand increases
muscles	• get shorter and fatter • more muscle fibres are ready for work • blood supply improves
skeleton	• bones become stronger • flexibility increases

KEY POINT

Overall the body becomes stronger, more flexible, able to withstand greater stress and recovers more quickly from hard physical activity.

The training programme

AQA A

EDEXCEL
OCR PE

WJEC
NICCEA

A training programme must meet the needs of the performer and relate to the game or activity that the individual is training for. It should be carefully planned to be carried out over a prolonged period of time. This planning should aim to achieve climax at competition time and take into account the close season of any activity.

Remember SPIRe:
- **S = Suitability**
- **P = Preparation**
- **I = In season**
- **Re = Recuperation**

There are **four** issues to be considered when planning a training programme.

1. **Suitability** for training – individuals must ensure that they are capable of following a sustained training programme. They must be free from injury and illness, have access to training facilities and have a genuine desire to improve their performance.
2. **Preparation** – **off-season** or **out-of-season** training should concentrate on maintaining a basic fitness level, aim to attain the correct body weight for the chosen sporting activity and include the acquisition of any essential skills. **Pre-season training** should include the progressive development of the energy systems, through both aerobic and anaerobic work, the development of strength and the practice of team-play situations.
3. **In-season** – **competition training** should aim to maintain fitness and skill levels, fluctuating in intensity so that the performer can peak at different times (relating to major events) throughout the season. Training should rise to a peak and then be followed by a number of rest days just before major competitions.
4. **Recuperation** – **post-season training** should not be overlooked. At the end of the competitive season it is essential that the performer continues with a light training programme to allow the body to recover from the stresses and strains of the season. It is at this time that more serious injuries should be dealt with prior to the start of off-season work.

You should be able to describe a training programme for a sport that you know well.

PROGRESS CHECK

1. Give three reasons for doing a warm-up before starting physical activity.
2. What are the main parts of a training session?
3. Explain why rest days are important in training programmes.
4. What is 'blood pooling' and when might it occur?

1. Prepare the mind and body for work, increase blood supply to the muscles, prepare the joints to work over a greater range. 2. Warm-up, training activity, cool down, rest. 3. So that muscles can recover from minor injuries. 4. The concentration of blood in the muscles which can happen if no cool-down period takes place after hard physical work.

Sample GCSE questions

Tim wants to improve his cardiovascular endurance.

(a) Should he train aerobically or anaerobically to achieve this?

aerobically

[1]

(b) Which of the following is the most appropriate training method to improve his cardiovascular endurance: weight training, interval, continuous?

continuous

Continuous training is sometimes called LSD.

[1]

At one of his training sessions Tim records his heart rate before exercise and for several minutes after exercise in order to look at his recovery rate.

(c) Explain what is meant by the term 'recovery rate'?

This is the time taken for the heart to return to its normal resting rate.

Remember that it is the heart, not the body that is returning to rest.

[1]

(d) What information would Tim gain by measuring his recovery rate?

his fitness level

It will also indicate any changes in his fitness level.

[1]

At the end of each training session Tim finishes with a 'cool down'.

(e) Give **two** examples of activities he might include in a 'cool down'.

jogging/walking, stretching

[2]

(f) **(i)** Give **two** physical reasons why you should 'cool down' at the end of a training session

maintain circulation, remove lactic acid, aid delivery of oxygen, re-stretch muscles after work

Although there are a number of possible answers, give only the number that you are asked for. Extra answers will not gain extra marks. Also, try to link part (i) with part (ii).

(ii) Explain why the reasons given above are important.

prevents fainting or dizziness, blood pooling, reduces chances of lactic acid build-up, prevents muscle stiffness

[2]

EDEXCEL 1999 Paper 1 Q31

Exam practice questions

(a) Give **one** physical advantage of training.

.... **[1]**

(b) Give **two** features of Fartlek training.

(i) ....

(ii) .... **[2]**

(c) Give **three** ways of reducing the risk of injury when taking part in sport and physical activity.

(i) ....

(ii) ....

(iii) .... **[3]**

(d) Outline the different injuries that could happen to the knee joint whilst taking part in sport and physical activity. Give reasons for your answer.

....

....

....

.... **[4]**

(e) Define the principle of overload.

....

....

....

....

....

.... **[5]**

AQA 1998 QA4

Chapter 4

Skill

The following topics are covered in this chapter:

- *Types of skill*
- *Contributions to performance*

4.1 Types of skill

LEARNING SUMMARY

After completing this section you should be able to:

- *define skill*
- *know the difference between basic and complex skills, and open and closed skills*
- *know the basic information processing models*

Skill defined

AQA A AQA B EDEXCEL WJEC NICCEA

Be able to define skill.

What is skill? One of the best definitions of skill is 'the **learned** ability to bring about **predetermined** results with maximum certainty, often with the **minimum outlay** of time, or energy, or both'.

The important parts of this definition are discussed below.

- **Learned** – a skill is something that is learned. Although some people seem to perform a skill naturally, all physical skills have to be learned.
- **Predetermined** – a skill has a result that is anticipated. The outcome of a skill action is expected by the performer.
- **Minimum outlay** – a skill, once it is learned correctly, is performed with the minimum of effort. So, a skill uses the components of fitness efficiently. There is a control of physical movement.

KEY POINT

Skill is learned, predetermined and involves the minimum outlay of effort.

Basic and complex skills, open and closed skills

AQA A AQA B EDEXCEL WJEC NICCEA

Basic and complex skills

Basic skills are best described as physical skills that:

- you learn at an early age, i.e. jumping and throwing
- are easily transferred to a number of situations, i.e. running in different ways
- form the basis for more complex skills, i.e. seat drop is the basis of swivel hips on the trampoline

Complex skills are best described as physical skills that:

- are specific to a given sport but not to any other sport, i.e. a serve in tennis
- need much practice to learn correctly, i.e. they may be made up of a number of basic skills

Be able to break down complex skills from your chosen sports.

In tennis, for example, the serve is described as a complex skill. It is made up from a number of basic skills. These are:

- holding the racket correctly
- being able to throw a ball in the air correctly
- being able to hit something above your head correctly
- being able to direct the ball to a specific point when it is hit

All these basic skills have to be learned and practised before they are put together to produce the complex skill of serving.

Open and closed skills

Skills are often described by the amount of control that the individual has over the timing of the performance. This is called **pacing**.

In some situations, such as when performing the tennis serve mentioned above, the performer will have full control over **when** the skill will be performed. This is called **internal** or **self-pacing** – the player decides when to serve.

In other situations, such as when paddling a canoe down a white water slalom course, external forces will affect when the paddling skill has to be performed. This is called **external pacing**. Rocks and waves determine when the canoeist will paddle.

Pacing has a bearing on whether a skill is described as an open or closed skill.

You must be able to differentiate between open and closed skills.

- **Open skills** are those which are most influenced by **external** factors. Deciding when to perform a tackle in a football or a hockey game depends as much on the actions of other players as on the ability to tackle.
- **Closed skills** follow a set, predetermined pattern of movement, regardless of any external factors. The archer, not his target, decides when to fire the arrow.

Not all skills fall into these two extreme categories: some may be regarded as part open and part closed. A forehand in badminton falls into both categories: it depends on your opponent hitting the shuttle to you (an external influence) but you decide whether to play the shot early or late. All skills fall somewhere along the line of the skill pendulum (see Fig 4.1).

Fig 4.1 The skill pendulum

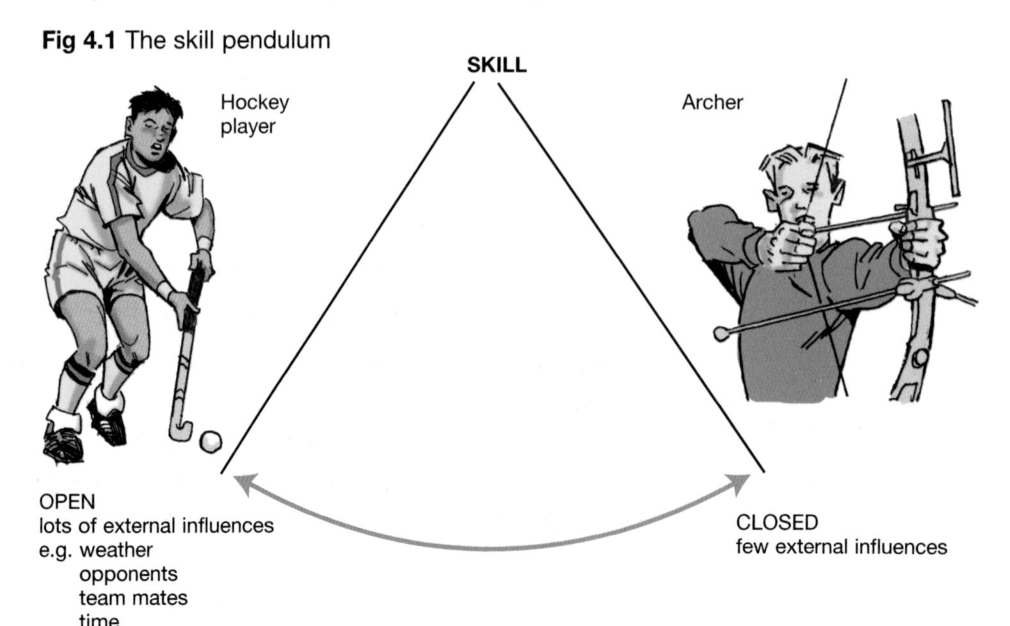

You should be able to describe and give examples of skills that are:
- open
- closed
- basic
- complex
- externally paced
- self-paced

Information processing models

AQA A AQA B EDEXCEL WJEC NICCEA

The nervous system

All movement is controlled by the **nervous system** of the body. This is made up of the:

1. **brain**
2. **brain stem**
3. **spinal cord**
4. **nerves** or **neurones**

The first **three** parts listed above are often called the **Central Nervous System** (**CNS**). It is here that all decisions are made (see Fig 4.2).

Fig 4.2 Nervous system

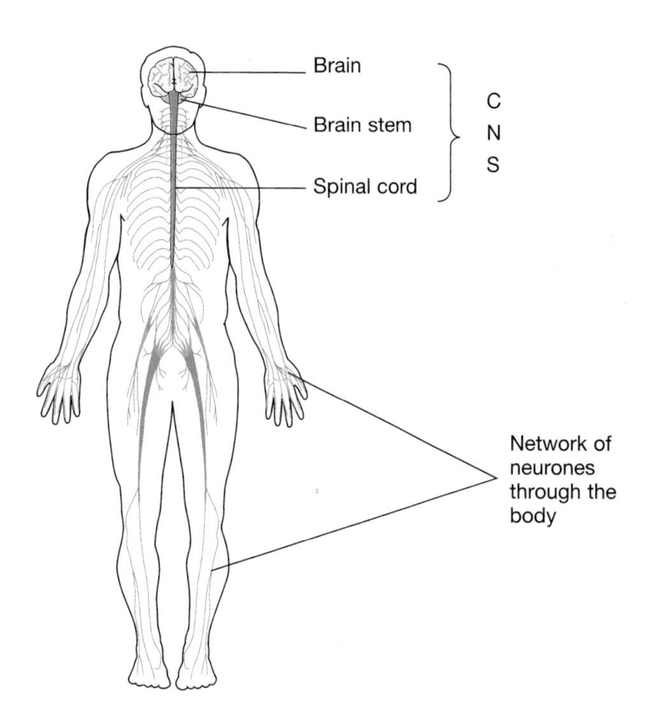

Receiving information and acting on it

Know the difference between sensory and effector nerves.

There are **two** kinds of nerves.

- **Sensory nerves** carry information to the CNS.
- **Effector nerves** carry information away from the CNS.

Know the difference between exterioceptors, proprioceptors and interioceptors.

Sensory nerves obtain information from outside the body via **exterioceptors**, such as the ears, eyes and skin. They also obtain information from within the body from **proprioceptors** such as the stretch receptors of muscles. **Interioceptors** provide information on the internal state of the body, such as how fast the heart is beating or how full the bladder is.

The way information is received and acted upon follows a set pattern as shown in Fig 4.3.

Fig 4.3 Information receipt and action pattern

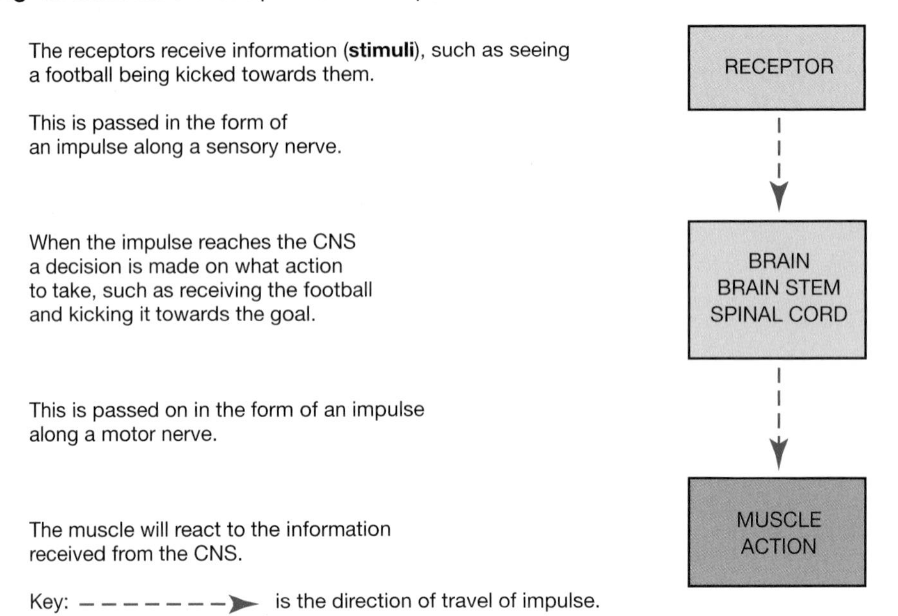

The speed at which a decision is made is called the **reaction time**. Knowing **how** to perform a skill is important, but knowing **when** to perform a skill is equally important. As your opponent serves in tennis, you receive lots of information through your eyes and ears, and from within your body. These different types of information are called **stimuli** (singular **stimulus**), and they are passed on to the CNS before any action is taken.

Remember that the CNS is part of the Nervous System.

So, information from outside the body (about your opponent's serve) is detected by the exterioceptors in the eyes and ears. At the same time, the CNS will be receiving stimuli from the proprioceptors within your body. These tell you what position your body is in as you prepare to receive the serve.

All this received information – these stimuli – is described as the **input**, and any action you take is called the **output**. Once the input has been received, you have to make decisions about **what** the output should be and **when** the output should take place. This process is called the **information processing model** (see Fig 4.4).

Fig 4.4 The simple information processing model

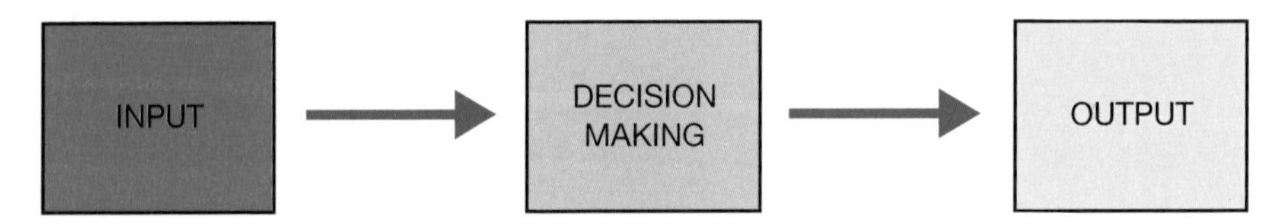

Feedback and performance

You should be aware of the importance of feedback in the information processing model.

The skilled performer will be able to adjust the output as it is being performed or as it is being repeated. The adjustment is often made on the basis of a **knowledge of results** or a **knowledge of performance**. This is called **feedback**.

- If an output has the desired effect – i.e. if we hit the target when shooting an arrow – we will try to repeat the same process in order to get the same results. This is knowledge of results.
- By the same token, we sometimes perform a physical skill and, regardless of its outcome, we know that it 'feels right'. This is **knowledge of performance**.

Both types of feedback can affect the output (see Fig 4.5).

Fig 4.5 The information processing model

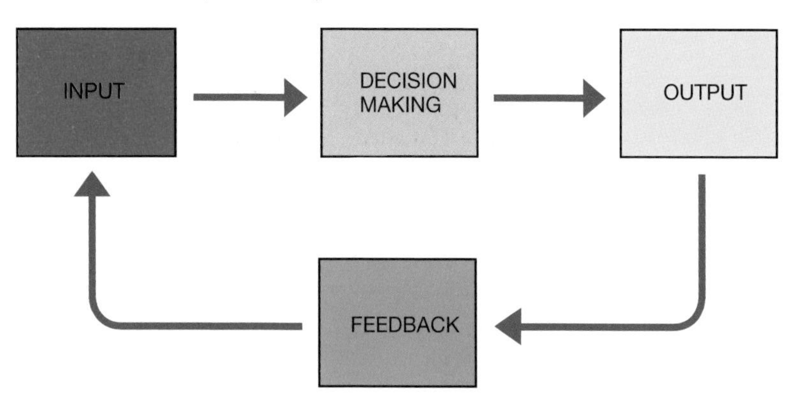

The interpretation of received stimuli by our brains is called **perception**. When perception takes place, inputs are checked against known remembered patterns of stimuli before a decision about output is made. This checking is carried out very quickly in the memory stores of the CNS (see Fig 4.6).

Fig 4.6 The extended information processing model

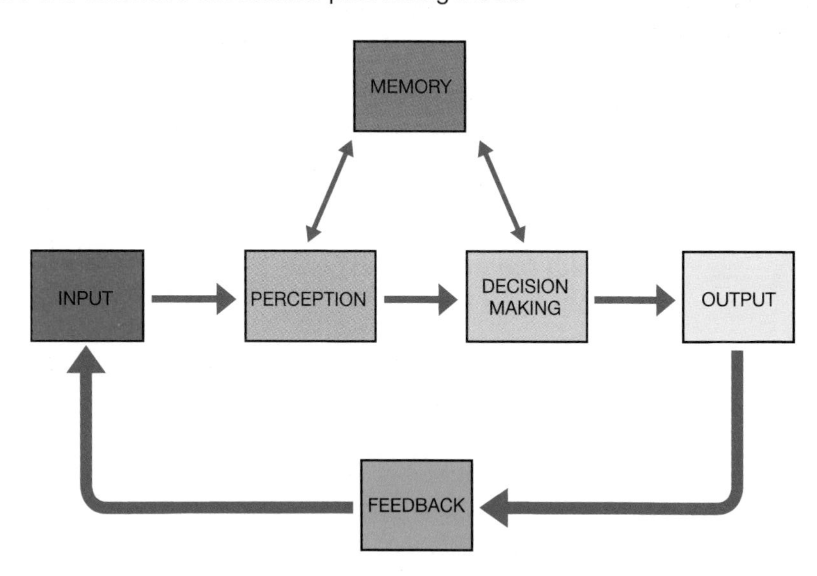

You should be able to draw diagrams of all the information processing models described.

KEY POINT **Note how we have built up the information processing model.**

We should remember that, when our senses receive information, we often take in more stimuli than we need to. The footballer taking the penalty kick needs to know where the ball is, where the keeper is and where the goal is. He may also be aware of the noise of the crowd behind the goal and the flashing of cameras. These extra, unwanted stimuli could overload his information processing capabilities.

However, since our brains can only can deal with a limited amount of stimuli, a selection process takes place. This part of the processing model is called **limited channel capacity**: some information is allowed through; other information is not (see Fig 4.7).

Fig 4.7 Limited channel capacity in the information processing model

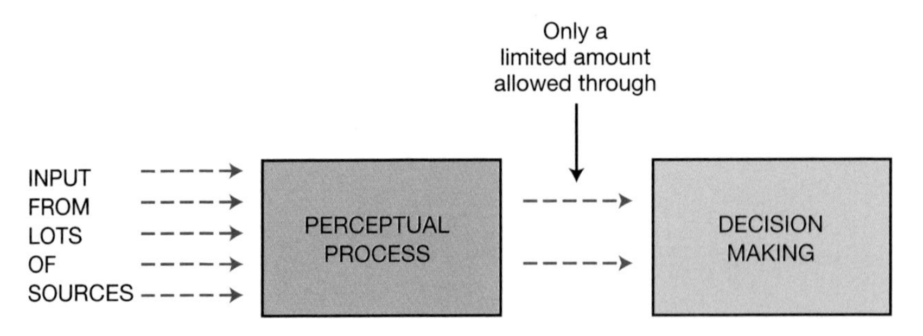

PROGRESS CHECK

1. Define skill.
2. What factors have the greatest influence on open skills?
3. What effect does feedback have on performance?
4. What is perception?

1. The learned ability to bring about predetermined results with maximum certainty, often with the minimum outlay of time or energy or both. 2. Open skills are most influenced by many external factors. 3. Feedback helps to correct performance. 4. Perception is the interpretation of stimuli.

4.2 Contributions to performance

After completing this section you should be able to:

- ***explain the effects of motivation and arousal on performance***
- ***explain goal setting***
- ***explain which components of skill are related to fitness***

Motivation and arousal

Motivation

Motivation is the amount of desire or enthusiasm that a person has for a given physical performance. This can influence how well or how badly an individual will perform. There are two types.

1. **Intrinsic motivation** is when a person motivates him or herself – the desire to succeed comes from within.
2. **Extrinsic motivation** is when a person's desire to succeed is stimulated by the chance of winning a trophy or prize – a reward from outside the performer.

KEY POINT

This is **positive motivation** – **negative motivation** can hinder performance.

Arousal

Your level of **arousal** can be described as how prepared you are to take part in an event. How keen you are to take part can influence how hard you might try to win. Unfortunately, it is possible to **over-arouse** a competitor. Too much arousal can lead to **anxiety** and excessive **stress**, causing a decrease in performance standards. Fig 4.8 represents what is called the **Inverted U Theory** of arousal.

Fig 4.8 Graph showing arousal level compared to performance level

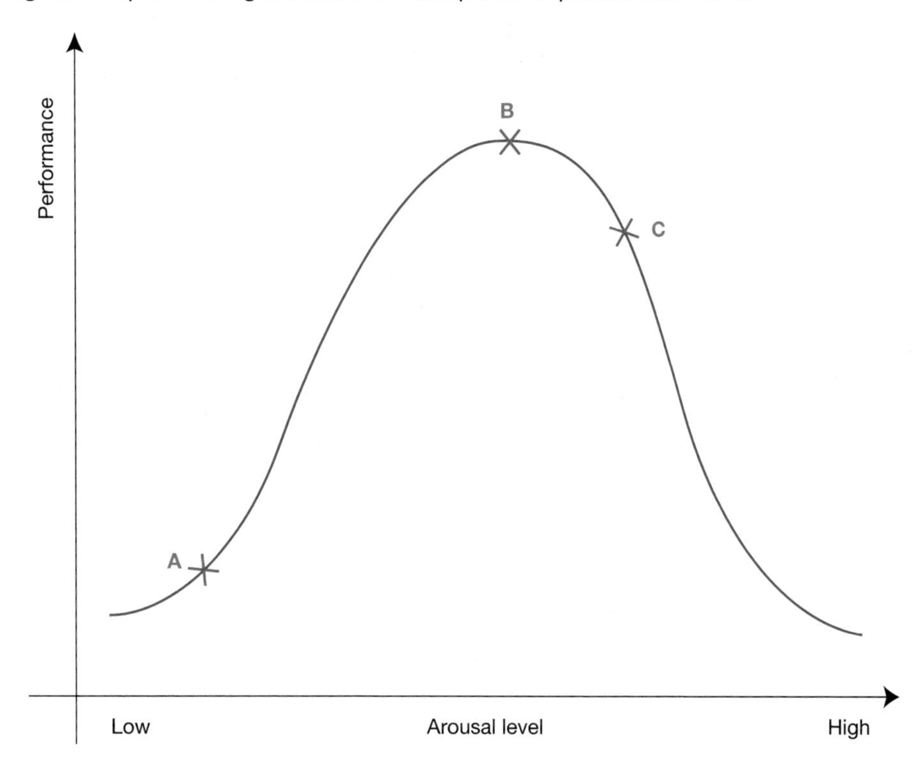

You should be able to explain the Inverted U Theory.

At point **A** on the graph there is little arousal and so the performance level is not raised. At point **B** the arousal level is at a middle level and performance is at its best. At point **C**, however, the arousal level has become so high that anxiety and stress are having a negative effect on performance, the standard of which is beginning to decrease. At this stage the performer is said to be 'psyched out': a person cannot give of their best in this situation.

Goal setting

AQA A

WJEC
NICCEA

Goal setting means devising **attainable targets**, which can help in the training process. These interim targets or goals are designed to lead to an ultimate long-term goal, such as winning an Olympic Gold Medal. The long-term goal is broken down into short and medium-term goals so the performer can see that success is within reach. So, these goals are like small stepping stones to the ultimate long-term goal.

Goal setting helps training because regular success builds up confidence and helps increase motivation. There is a **SMARTER** way to remember short and medium-term goals!

It is worth learning this mnemonic.

- **S – specific** to the long-term target
- **M – measurable**, so that progress can be seen
- **A – agreed** between coach and the individual
- **R – realistic**, i.e. attainable
- **T – time-phased** to fit into the long-term goal
- **E – exciting**, just like the ultimate goal
- **R – recorded** so that progress can be seen

KEY POINT **Be aware of the importance of motivation, arousal and goal setting in performance.**

The components of skill that are related to fitness

AQA A AQA B EDEXCEL OCR PE OCR G WJEC NICCEA

KEY POINT **Skill contributes to performance just as physical fitness does.**

Just as physical fitness has a number of components (see Chapter 2), skill also has a number of aspects. Each of these components can affect the performance of physical activities. The main components are:

- **Agility** – this is the ability to change the position of the body, to change direction and be in precise control of all movements when they are done at speed. This particular skill is very important in activities such as rugby, trampolining and gymnastics. Agility can be developed through practice which is related to the sport, for example, set movement patterns can be learned.
- **Balance** – this is the ability to maintain a given posture in static and dynamic situations. Static balance is important in activities such as gymnastics, e.g. when performing a hand stand. Dynamic balance is the ability to maintain a balance under changing conditions of posture, as the gymnast does on the balance beam.
- **Co-ordination** – this is the ability to perform smooth and accurate physical tasks involving the use of the senses. The performer's body must be able to move precisely and smoothly when responding to changing situations, such as when bowling in cricket.
- **Reaction** – this is the ability of the body, or a body part, to respond to a given stimulus. An example of this is the amount of time it takes to react to the sound of a starting gun. This reaction time includes the time between the gun sounding and the detection of the sound by the senses.
- **Timing** – this is the ability to co-ordinate movements in relation to external factors. This can be explained if we consider the spike in volleyball. The spiker can see the ball being set in readiness for the spike, but it is the spiker who has to time his or her jump and arm swing correctly in order to perform the action. The jump and arm swing must coincide with the position of the ball just above the net.

Reaction time is not to be confused with response time, which is the time taken to respond to to the detected stimulus (the gun's sound) and start moving.

These components of skill which are related to fitness can all be learned and practised. The performer's acquisition of these skills can also be tested (see Chapter 5).

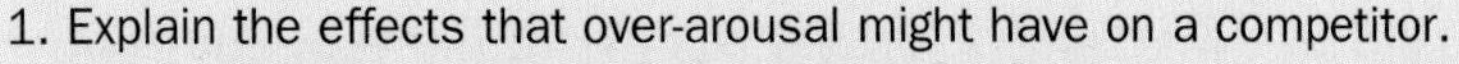

1. Explain the effects that over-arousal might have on a competitor.
2. What should long-term goals be divided into?
3. Give a definition of agility.
4. Explain the term 'dynamic balance'.

1. It can cause anxiety and stress, reducing performance levels. 2. Short and medium-term goals. 3. The ability to change the position of the body, to change direction and be in precise control of all movements when they are performed at speed. 4. The ability to maintain a balance under changing (moving) conditions of posture.

Sample GCSE questions

Skills can be classified on various continuums. The pacing continuum classifies the skills by the extent to which the performer has control over the timing of the action.

self-paced ———————————— externally paced

1. State a sport, or an action from a sport, that is self-paced.

Gymnastic activities can be done quickly or slowly; the gymnast has control over these.

[1]

Any suitable sport or an action from any sport can be used. The important part is to show that you realise the performer must decide the timing.

2. State a sport, or an action from a sport, that is externally paced.

In team games such as football and hockey the timing of the action is often dictated by what is happening around the player.

[1]

In this case the timing is not decided solely by the player.

The diagram shows the stages of processing information.

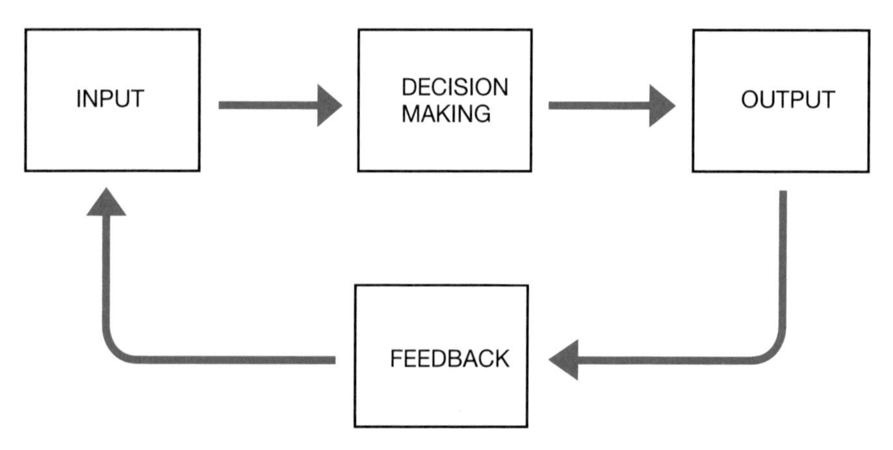

3. State and explain the **three** different ways in which the brain receives information (input) during a game.

Exterioceptors, such as the eye, provide information: for example, where the ball is, where team mates are and where the opposition is.

Proprioceptors in the inner ear provide information on the position of the head; those in muscles, tendons and joints provide information on muscle tension, how stretched the muscles are and on the angle of the joint.

Interioceptors provide information on the workings of the body systems: for example, on how hard the heart is working and how fast or deeply one is breathing.

[6]

Two marks are awarded for each answer. This means that two pieces of information are needed for each answer. Space is provided for this.

NICCEA 1999 Paper 1 Q24 & 25

Exam practice questions

(a) To what aspect of skill-related fitness does each of A, B and C refer?

A ....

B ....

C .... **[3]**

(b) State the type of movement in the somersault in Diagram A.

.... **[1]**

(c) **(i)** Define reaction time.

....

.... **[2]**

(ii) Give **one** example from any physical activity of your choice where good reaction time would be of benefit.

....

....

.... **[1]**

EDEXCEL 1998 Specimen Paper Q29

Measurement in sport

The following topics are covered in this chapter:

- ***The value of testing in sport***
- ***Tests for strength***
- ***Tests for suppleness***
- ***Tests for stamina***
- ***Tests for cardiovascular fitness***
- ***Tests for skill-related fitness***
- ***Combination tests for physical fitness***

5.1 The value of testing in sport

After studying this section you should be able to:

- ***explain why testing takes place in sport***
- ***explain how testing takes place in sport and know the value of data obtained***

Why do we test?

It can be argued that measurement is taking place in sport all the time. At the most simplistic level this includes counting the **score** in a game of football or badminton. The score shows which individual or team has the most points and is, therefore, the more able.

When successive games are played against a number of opponents, the scores from each game can indicate which player or team is the most able overall, and whether teams have improved their performance.

On a more complex level, it is possible to measure the effects that specific types of training have on the individual. This allows us to establish, for example, how fit, strong or supple they are.

Any aspect of fitness can be tested if the right test is available.

By testing an individual **before** they start a training programme, it is possible to identify those physical deficiencies that need to be improved to attain fitness. Repeated testing can indicate levels of **progression** during a training programme.

In all tests it is important to ensure that the test measures what it sets out to measure. This is called **validity**, i.e. a test for arm strength should not include the use of the leg muscles.

Know the meanings of the technical terms related to testing.

After a test has been carried out some results will have been obtained. The results of the test are called **data**. This data may be illustrated in the form of a graph, bar chart or pie chart, and should always be studied closely. This close inspection is called the **analysis** of the data. By analysing the data it is possible to draw **conclusions** about, for example, how effective the training programme is, or how strong one person is compared to another.

Sometimes tests come with a list of **norms**. These are sets of figures that indicate, in general terms, how fit or strong or supple an individual might be compared with a sample of people of the same age. Care must be taken when comparing individual scores with norms: such comparisons are crude and not definitive.

How do we test? What do the data tell us?

AQA A AQA B EDEXCEL WJEC NICCEA

Test protocols

Whenever a test is used it should be carried out in the correct way. The correct method is called the **test protocol**. If this is not followed, the results might be incorrect. The rest of this chapter describes some aspects of test protocols (the ways to carry out tests).

This warning is most important.

The person being tested is sometimes called the testee.

KEY POINT

WARNING
No test should be attempted unless:
- **a suitably qualified person is present**
- **the person being tested is medically fit to take the test**
- **a suitable warm-up has taken place before testing starts**

The value of test data

Data obtained from any test should indicate the quality of that performance, i.e. how good or poor that person's performance was compared to others who have completed the same test (or compared to that person's previous results). Although comparisons can be made between different people's test results, it should be remembered that any results obtained from physical tests are only an **indication** of the status of the individual. Results can be influenced by many factors, especially test protocol.

PROGRESS CHECK

Explain the following terms:
1. validity
2. data
3. norms
4. protocol

1. The test measures what it sets out to measure. 2. Scores obtained from a test. 3. Sets of figures that indicate, in general terms, how fit or strong or supple an individual might be compared with a sample of people of the same age. 4. The way a test should be carried out.

5.2 Tests for strength

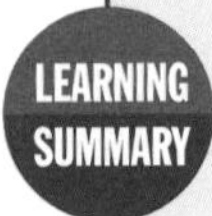

After studying this section you should be able to:

- *describe tests for strength*

Some recognised tests

NICCEA

Measuring strength in the hand and forearm

A grip dynamometer is used. The testee grips and squeezes as hard as possible (see Photo 5.1).

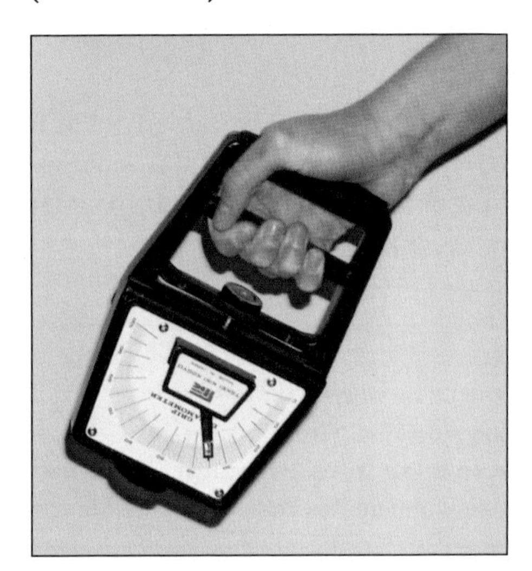

Photo 5.1 Grip dynamometer

Before using a dynamometer, make sure that the pointer is set at zero. A measurement is taken from the dial.

Measuring leg and back strength

A **tensiometer** is used for this. Although this piece of equipment is easy to use, it must be used correctly. When pulling on the handles, the back must be kept upright and straight (see Fig 5.1).

Fig 5.1 Using a tensiometer to measure leg and back strength

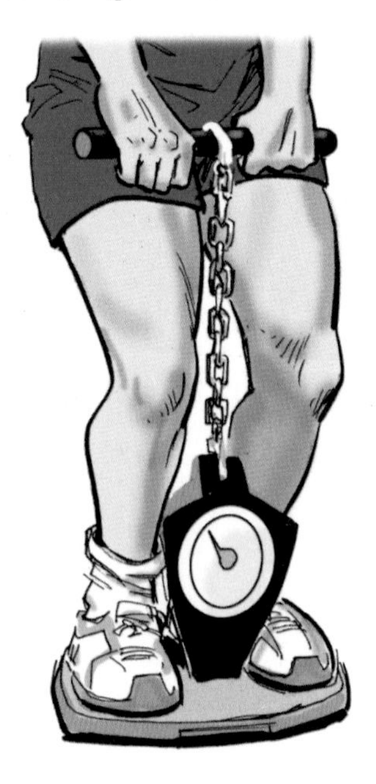

Before using a tensiometer, make sure that the pointer is set at zero. The measurement is taken from the dial.

Measuring power

Power is a combination of speed and strength. This can be measured by using either the standing high jump or the standing long jump tests. These are tests of **explosive strength** (see Figs 5.2 and 5.3).

Fig 5.2 Standing high jump

The subject faces the wall and stretches both arms above their head with their hands side by side, so that the fingertip level whilst standing can be marked. The subject then turns sideways to wall and with both feet together jumps as high as possible to touch the board with the fingertips of one outstretched hand. The subject may swing their arms before jumping if desired. The distance jumped is the distance between the two marks.

Fig 5.3 Standing long jump

The subject stands on a non-slip surface, usually a gymnastics mat, marked with a straight line. The subject performs a two-footed jump along the mat. The subject may swing their arms before jumping if desired. The distance jumped is measured from the start line to the back of the rearmost heel.

5.3 Tests for suppleness

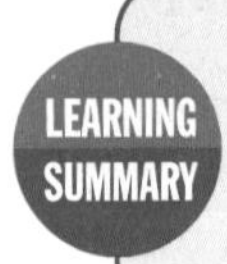

After studying this section you should be able to:

- ***describe tests for suppleness***

Some recognised tests

These tests tend to be localised. They measure the suppleness for just **one part** of the body.

Shoulder lift

This test measures flexibility at the shoulder joint (see Fig 5.4).

Fig 5.4 The shoulder lift

The subject lies on the floor, face down, grasps a short stick with both hands, with hands held shoulder width apart. The short stick is raised as high as possible with arms straight and chin touching the ground. The distance is the height the stick is raised from the ground.

Sit-and-reach test

This test measures suppleness in the back and hamstrings (see Fig 5.5).

Fig 5.5 Sit-and-reach test

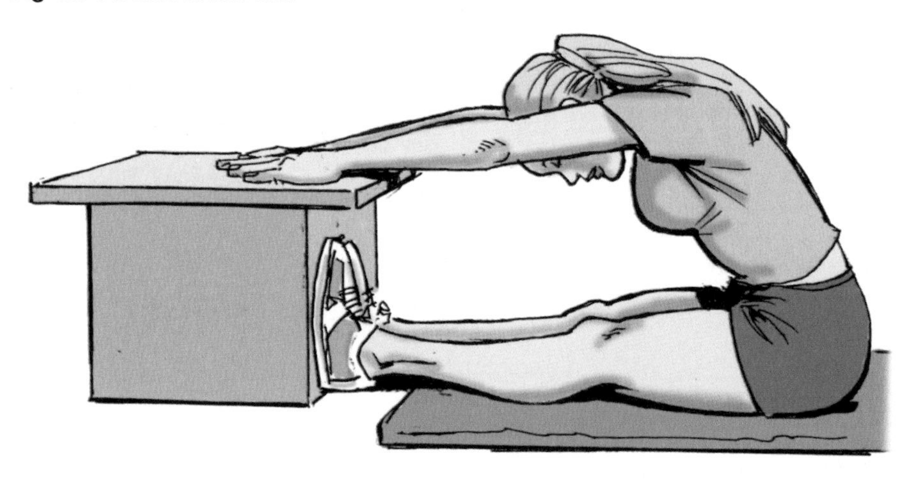

The subject sits on floor with legs fully extended and feet flexed, hands touching the sit-and-reach box. The subject then stretches forward with both hands, keeping the legs straight, sliding palms along the box. The measurement is the distance the fingertips reach beyond the toes. If the subject cannot reach beyond the toes, then the distance from the fingertips to the toes is measured. This is recorded as a negative score. **Note** that subject must not jerk forward, but should stretch forward in an even manner.

Trunk extension

This test measures the suppleness of the lower back (see Fig 5.6).

Fig 5.6 Trunk extension

The subject lies face down on the floor with both hands clasped behind the head. The head and shoulders are raised as high as possible, while the feet remain in contact with the ground. The measurement is the distance from the floor to the point of the chin.

5.4 Tests for stamina

LEARNING SUMMARY

After studying this section you should be able to:

- ***describe tests for local muscular stamina***

Some recognised tests

AQA A AQA B EDEXCEL WJEC NICCEA

The following tests are for local muscular stamina. They test specific muscle groups.

Press-ups

These measure arm and body strength (see Fig 5.7).

Fig 5.7 Press-ups

These should always be completed with the back straight. Sometimes girls with reduced arm strength adjust the front support position and pivot round the knees rather than the feet. Even so, the back must be kept straight. Measurement is the maximum number of press-ups completed.

Sit-ups

These measure the strength and endurance of the abdominal muscles (see Fig 5.8).

Fig 5.8 Sit-ups

The subject lies flat on their back on a mat with hands clasped behind the head, knees at right angles, both feet flat on the floor and slightly apart. The subject then sits up to touch knees with elbows and then returns to the starting position. A partner holds the subject's ankles to make sure feet stay on the floor. The measurement is the total number of sit-ups completed.

Fig 5.9 Pull-ups or chins

Pull-ups or chins

These measure the strength and endurance of the upper arm, especially biceps and shoulder girdle (see Fig 5.9).

The subject holds onto a beam or rings, using the underhand grip, with feet clear of the floor. The chin is raised above the beam and then the arms are fully extended. The measurement is the number of times the chin is raised above the beam after a full arm extension.

Fig 5.10 Dips

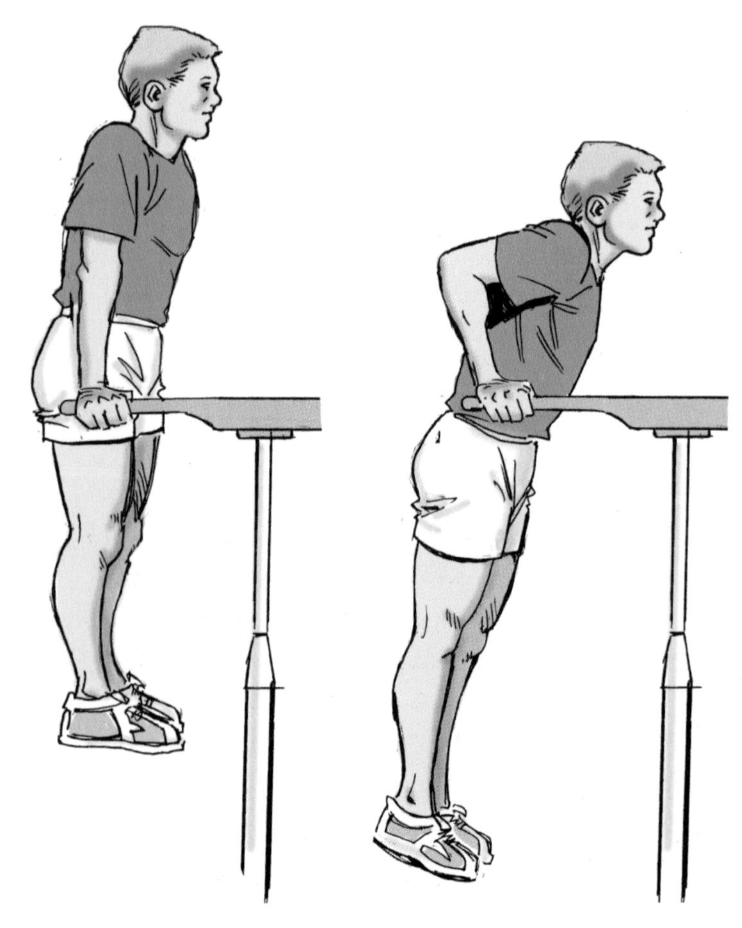

Dips

These measure the strength and endurance of the upper arm, especially triceps and shoulder girdle (see Fig 5.10).

The subject supports their full body weight on both hands with the arms fully extended. The hands are placed on suitable bars located shoulder width apart. The body is lowered until the elbow bends to a 90° angle. Then the arms are fully extended. The measurement is the number of dips followed by a full arm extension.

5.5 Tests for cardiovascular fitness

After studying this section you should be able to:

- *describe tests for cardiovascular fitness*

Some recognised tests

Cardiovascular fitness is often referred to as **cardiovascular stamina**, **aerobic power** or **aerobic capacity**.

Harvard step test

In this test a subject steps onto and off a bench or sturdy box 45 cm high (see Fig 5.11).

Fig 5.11 Harvard step test

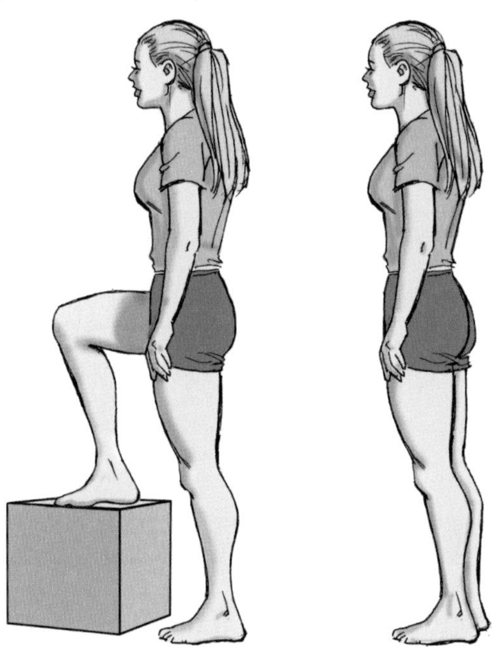

The subject steps fully onto and off the bench for 5 minutes at a rate of 30 steps per minute. At the end of the exercise, after a 1-minute rest, the pulse rate is counted for 30 seconds. The pulse rate is then doubled (to give a rate per minute). This is often described as a **sub-maximal test** because the activity rate is predetermined – the subject doesn't have to try to reach a personal maximum rate.

This is only a simple formula. Other, more complex formulae can be used but they require many more readings.

A fitness rating is obtained by using the following formula:

$$\frac{100 \times 300 \text{ (length of the exercise in seconds)}}{5.5 \times \text{number of heart beats per minute}}$$

12-minute run test

This is also known as the **Cooper test**. In this test, the subject runs and/or walks as far as possible in 12 minutes. This is often described as a **maximal test** (i.e. the subject covers as much ground as possible in the time allowed). The fitness level is established by comparing the distance run to established norms for the test.

Progressive shuttle run test

This test is also known as the **bleep test** or the **multi-stage fitness test**. The subject runs continuous shuttle runs between two lines drawn 20 metres apart. The pace is established by a tape recording that sounds a bleep at the end of each leg of the shuttle run. As the test progresses, the time between the bleeps gets shorter and a level is indicated. When three bleeps in a row are missed the fitness level of the subject has been established. This also is a **maximal test**.

Sub-maximal test work is to a specific level.
Maximal test work is to the best of your ability.

5.6 Tests for skill-related fitness

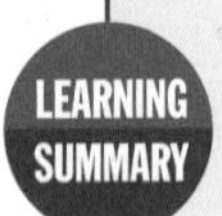

After studying this section you should be able to describe tests for:

- *agility*
- *reaction*
- *speed*
- *balance*
- *co-ordination*

Agility

The Illinois Agility Run

Agility is a combination of **speed** and **co-ordination**. Both these aspects have to be tested in a protocol which measures agility. The Illinois Agility Run combines a test for running with one for the ability to change direction around a series of cones set out in a predetermined pathway (see Fig 5.12).

Fig 5.12 Layout of Illinois Agility Run

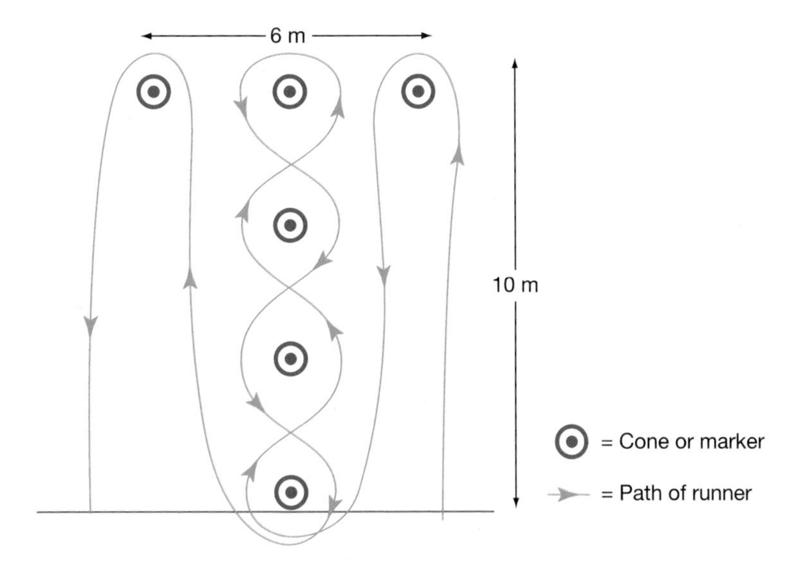

The subject starts by lying face-down behind the start line with their chin on the floor. On the command 'Go', the subject stands up and runs round the cones following the prescribed pathway, travelling as fast as possible. The measurement is the time taken to complete the run. This can be compared to established norms.

Reaction

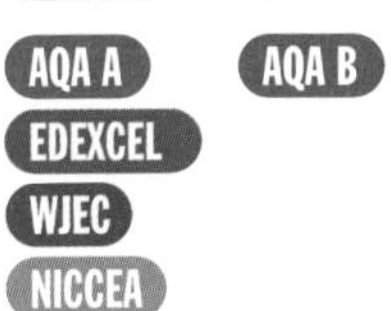

Metre rule drop test

A metre rule is held against a flat wall and the subject stands with their thumb alongside, but **not touching**, the 0 cm mark. Without warning, the ruler is dropped and must be caught by gripping between the thumb and index finger (see Fig 5.13).

Fig 5.13 Metre rule drop test

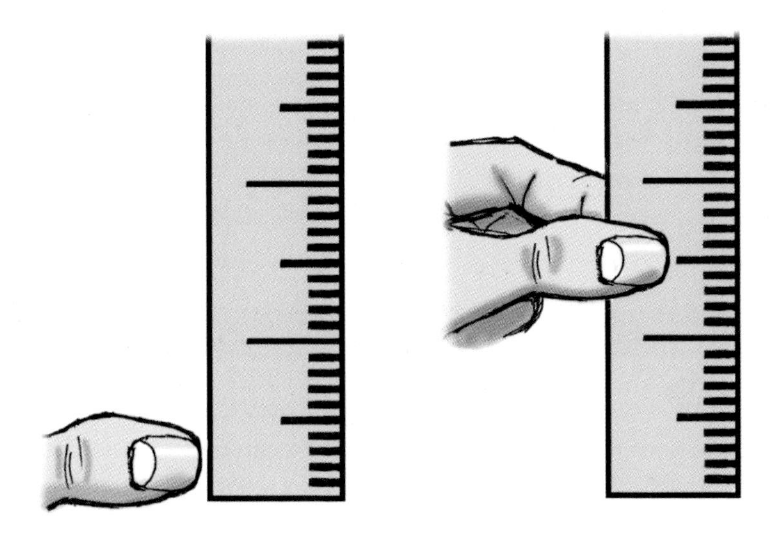

The measurement is the distance between top of the ruler and thumb/index finger.

Speed, balance and co-ordination

AQA A AQA B EDEXCEL WJEC NICCEA

Speed

Timed run

Speed can be tested simply by timing a run over an agreed distance, usually less than 100 metres. Distances are run in shuttles of around 10 metres and are usually completed indoors. As protocols for this test vary, it is not always possible to compare times with established norms. Measurement is made with a stop watch.

Balance

Stork stand test

The subject stands on one foot and places the other foot against the inside of the knee. The hands are placed on the hips. Timing starts when both eyes are closed and stops when eyes open, foot parts from knee or the subject loses their balance.

Co-ordination

Tennis ball catch

The subject stands 2 metres from a wall and tosses a tennis ball underarm against the wall from one hand and catches it with the opposite hand. This action is repeated with throw and catch being continuous. Measurement is the total number of catches made in 30 seconds.

5.7 Combination tests for physical fitness

LEARNING SUMMARY

After studying this section you should be able to:

- *describe the JCR test*
- *describe the JCD test*

JCR test

AQA A AQA B EDEXCEL WJEC NICCEA

Know a test for physical fitness and its protocol.

This test combines scores for standing high jump, number of completed chins and the time taken to complete a 100 metre run. Scores are compared with established tables and a fitness level is indicated.

KEY POINT

JCR = Jump, Chins, Run.

JCD test

AQA A AQA B EDEXCEL WJEC NICCEA

This test combines scores for standing high jump, number of completed chins and number of completed dips. Scores are compared with established tables and a fitness level is indicated.

KEY POINT

JCR = Jump, Chins, Dips.

Note that norms (where applicable) for the tests described in this section are given in the appendix.

PROGRESS CHECK

1. Name a test for each of the following:
   (i) hand and arm strength
   (ii) strength and endurance of abdominal muscles
   (iii) upper arm strength, especially triceps
2. Explain what the following tests measure:
   (i) standing high jump
   (ii) sit and reach test
3. Explain the difference between a maximal test and a sub-maximal test.

1. (i) Grip dynamometer (ii) sit-ups (iii) dips. 2. (i) Explosive leg strength (ii) suppleness of lower back and hamstrings. 3. Maximal test is work done to the best of your ability; sub-maximal test is work done to a specific level.

Sample GCSE questions

(a) What component of physical fitness would you be testing if you used a hand grip dynamometer?

strength of the hand/lower arm

[1]

(b) Give **two** reasons why it is important to follow correct procedures when carrying out fitness tests.

any two from: validity, safety, comparison

[2]

(c) **(i)** Name **two** recognised tests for cardiovascular endurance.

any two from: 12 minute (Cooper) run, Harvard step test, bleep/multi-stage fitness test

(ii) Describe fully the procedures carried out for each test.

describe the two tests from last question

Knowledge of protocol, distances and scoring system must be shown.

(iii) In some tests of cardiovascular endurance, taking a pulse rate is necessary. Why is this pulse rate a guide to basic cardiovascular fitness?

Good guides of cardiovascular endurance are: low resting heart rate, lower maximum heart rate, quicker return to resting heart rate after exercise.

Any one of these will gain marks.

[6]

Exam practice questions

(a) What physical component of fitness does the 'sit-and-reach' test measure?

.... **[1]**

(b) Suggest **three** reasons for testing physical fitness.

(i) ....

(ii) ....

(iii) .... **[3]**

(c) Describe fully how muscular strength and muscular endurance can be tested. Say what the main difference between the tests is.

....

....

.... **[3]**

(d) Name and describe a test of agility.

....

.... **[1]**

(e) Explain briefly why agility is an important physical component needed for a games player.

....

....

.... **[2]**

Factors affecting performance

The following topics are covered in this chapter:

- Food and diet
- Lifestyle
- Illness and injury
- Physical make-up
- Personal history
- Environmental conditions
- Drug use and abuse

KEY POINT: Remember FLIPPED stands for fitness!

6.1 Food and diet

LEARNING SUMMARY

After studying this section you should be able to:

- ***describe the components of a healthy diet***
- ***explain the importance of a balanced diet***
- ***describe the relationship between diet and exercise***
- ***describe how energy is produced***

Healthy diet

AQA A AQA B EDEXCEL OCR PE OCR G WJEC NICCEA

The essential components of a healthy diet are:

- fruit and vegetables
- cereals and grains
- eggs, cheese, meat and fish
- milk and other milk products

These food groups provide all the essential **nutrients** for the sports performer. These nutrient groups and their contribution to our energy requirements are shown in Table 6.1.

Be able to describe the main foodstuffs needed for a healthy diet.

Table 6.1 Essential nutrients

proteins	these provide approximately 15% of our energy
carbohydrates	these provide approximately 55% of our energy
fats	these provide approximately 30% of our energy
vitamins	only a small amount of these are needed
minerals	only a small amount of these are needed

The main sources of nutrients are listed below (see Table 6.2).

Table 6.2 Sources of nutrients

Be able to give examples of foodstuffs that contain proteins, carbohydrates, fats, and vitamins and minerals.

Nutrient	Source
proteins	found in meats, cheese, fish, eggs, soya, nuts
carbohydrates	found in flour foods (breads), sugar foods (jams), dried fruit
fats	found in milk products (butter, cream), lard, nuts, fish, meat
vitamins and minerals	found in the whole range of foodstuffs

Photo 6.1 Sources of proteins and vitamins

The main functions of nutrients are listed below (see Table 6.3).

Table 6.3 Functions of nutrients

Know the functions of proteins, carbohydrates, fats and vitamins and minerals.

Nutrient	Function
proteins	needed for growth, the building and repair of body cells
carbohydrates	provide energy
fats	provide energy and insulation, often stored under the skin
vitamins	help in the formation of bodily tissues (hair, teeth, skin, nails) and are necessary for all chemical reactions in the body
minerals	essential for the uptake of vitamins, the formation of bodily tissues and the carrying out of chemical reactions

Non-nutrients such as fibre and water are just as necessary as nutrients in a healthy diet.

The bulk of most fruit and vegetables is made up of **fibre**. This is essential to our diet although it is not a nutrient. It helps to keep the digestion system working.

High fibre foods usually provide little energy, but make you feel fuller. This can help in weight loss. (Weight loss should **always** be carefully monitored.)

Water is present in many foods and drinks, and is essential to our diet. Like fibre it is not a nutrient but is needed to replace liquids lost through sweating or passing of urine, and for the chemical reactions that take place in the body.

Balanced diet

AQA A | AQA B | EDEXCEL | OCR PE | OCR G | WJEC | NICCEA

Not all diets are healthy. The food taken in must provide all the nutrients for body growth and the energy for exercise. A balanced diet must contain all the nutrients you need in the correct amount. A varied diet must have a plentiful supply of fruit and vegetables and not contain too much fat (See Table 6.4).

- **excess food = increase in body fat**
- **insufficient food = no energy reserves**

Table 6.4 Balanced diet

Daily intake	EQUALS	energy expenditure	EQUALS	stable weight
Daily intake	GREATER THAN	energy expenditure	EQUALS	weight gain
Daily intake	LESS THAN	energy expenditure	EQUALS	weight loss

The relationship between diet and exercise

AQA A | AQA B | EDEXCEL | OCR PE | OCR G | WJEC | NICCEA

Before hard work do not overload the stomach.

Involvement in hard physical exercise does not seem to have any long-term effects on the digestive system. However, during hard physical exercise blood is diverted from the stomach to the working muscles. This means that any food in the stomach cannot be absorbed during the exercise. Often the body tries to get rid of this food during exercise by vomiting.

Diet is of major importance to the sportsperson. Different performers require different types of food, reflecting the different types of physical activity that are undertaken.

For example, a diet to provide muscle bulk is not the same as a diet to improve stamina.

- Sprinters and weightlifters require lots of **protein** for **muscle bulk**.
- Long distance runners require lots of **carbohydrate** for **endurance**.

In addition, a person's diet may change prior to competition. The aims of the pre-competition diet may be to:

- build up stores of carbohydrates – so that energy can be produced for longer periods of time (**carbohydrate loading**)
- enter the competition with as little in the stomach as possible – this helps the breathing process
- prevent gastric disturbances – the competitor should avoid gas-making foods such as onions, baked beans and cabbage
- provide a positive psychological attitude – if a good diet is followed it helps to develop a sense of well-being, both before and during competition (see Fig 6.1).

Fig 6.1 Ways to achieve carbohydrate loading

days before competition: 7	6	5	4	3	2	1		approx. rise in muscle glycogen
normal training diet and activity							competition day	normal
hard session	low carbohydrate diet			high carbohydrate diet				140% increase
		hard session		high carbohydrate				90% increase
				high carbohydrate				50% increase

> **If a meal is taken directly after activity, blood is directed to the stomach from the muscles, where it is still assisting in the recovery process (i.e. removal of lactic acid).**

- During physical activity foodstuffs must be avoided, but sportspeople should drink liquids – especially water – to replace losses brought about by sweating and energy production, and to help maintain body temperature.
- After hard physical activity it is important to continue replacing lost fluid, and eating food replaces depleted energy stores. However, eating should be delayed from between one to two hours after competition.

Post-competition diet should include early replacement of liquid to compensate for fluid loss, followed by ingestion of carbohydrates to help replace energy loss.

Diet and energy production

AQA A | AQA B | EDEXCEL | OCR PE | OCR G | WJEC | NICCEA

In order to walk or run, our muscles must be able to contract. To do this they need energy. Muscles get most of their energy when **glucose** and **oxygen** react together. Oxygen is obtained through the air by normal breathing. Glucose, however, comes from the food we eat.

> **Know this simple process.**

Foods such as bread, potatoes and rice contain **carbohydrate**.
↓
Carbohydrate is digested to form **glucose**.
↓
Glucose passes through the wall of the stomach into the **blood**.
↓
The blood carries some glucose to the **muscles**.
↓
The glucose is stored in the muscles as **glycogen**.
↓
The glycogen breaks down to glucose when the muscles work to produce **energy**.

> **Remember the glycogen storage areas.**

The blood also carries some glucose to be stored as glycogen in the **liver**. From here it can be released, when needed, to the muscles via the blood.

Muscles obtain energy for contraction from the breakdown of ATP into ADP. It is the process of glycolysis (breakdown of glucose) that produces enough energy to rebuild ATP from ADP so that muscle contraction can continue (see Fig 3.1).

So, oxygen and glucose react together to produce energy in the form of ATP. If a large and continuous supply of oxygen is available, then the energy is produced by the **aerobic system**. This works in the following way.

KEY POINT

glucose + oxygen = energy + two waste products (water and carbon dioxide)

The waste products are excreted:

- water in urine and sweat
- carbon dioxide by breathing out

During very hard physical exercise there is not enough oxygen for the aerobic system to produce energy. When this happens the **anaerobic system** is used.

KEY POINT

glucose = small amount of energy quickly + waste product (lactic acid)

Lactic acid can only be removed when it combines with oxygen. As there is not enough oxygen, lactic acid builds up, eventually forcing the muscles to stop working. This is described as an **oxygen debt**. The only way to get rid of this oxygen debt is to stop working and breathe in large amounts of oxygen. When the debt has been repaid, physical work can begin again.

PROGRESS CHECK

1. Name three components of a balanced diet.
2. For what purpose does the body use carbohydrates?
3. Explain the disadvantages of eating a meal just prior to a competition.
4. Name two sources of protein.

1. Any three from proteins, carbohydrates, fats, vitamins, minerals. 2. Energy providers. 3. During competition blood is diverted from the stomach to the working muscles, thus food cannot be absorbed. It can lead to under performance. The body will often try to get rid of food in such situations by vomiting. 4. Any two from meat, cheese, fish, eggs, soya, nuts.

6.2 Lifestyle

After studying this section you should be able to:

- *describe how lifestyle might affect performance*

The way we live affects our performance

AQA A | AQA B | EDEXCEL | OCR PE | OCR G | WJEC | NICCEA

Training for fitness not only includes doing the correct physical work, but also means generally living our lives in a healthy way. It is not possible to 'burn the candle at both ends' and produce a good class of performance.

So, what do we mean by our well-being? It covers:

- **physical** well-being – a body working well, free from illness and injury
- **mental** well-being – a relaxed attitude, a mind free from stress and worry
- **social** well-being – a warm, contented, well-fed existence in a settled social environment

KEY POINT

The most suitable lifestyle for an athlete is a healthy lifestyle. Healthy in this sense means taking account of our physical, mental and social well-being.

A person with a healthy lifestyle could be said to have a **SASHED** approach to life!

Be able to describe the SASHED approach to life.

- **Sleep** – sufficient good quality sleep is an essential part of any training programme.
- **Attitude** – a positive attitude is desirable in all people, but essential in a sportsperson. 'Attitude' includes having **respect** for one's opponents and fellow players. Like a positive approach to competition, respect for others is essential and it can help, indirectly, to produce a better individual performance.
- **Smoking** – smoking tobacco makes you smell, can ruin your health and can eventually kill you.

- **Hygiene** – good personal hygiene helps you to avoid infection and makes you feel good. For the athlete, good foot care is essential.

Verrucae are caused by a viral infection and athlete's foot is a fungal infection. They are spread by direct contact with socks, towels and wet changing room floors. To avoid infection, take care when walking in bare feet and make use of clean flip flops (or similar) that are disinfected regularly.

- **Environment** – living in a pollution-free situation can help to avoid respiratory illnesses. Also, climate and the weather can affect performance.
- **Diet** – a correctly balanced diet can help you cope with the everyday stresses of life.

1. List the three main stated types of well-being.
2. What does SASHED stand for?

1. Physical, mental, social. 2. Sleep. Attitude, Smoking, Hygiene, Environment, Diet.

6.3 Illness and injury

LEARNING SUMMARY

After studying this section you should be able to:

- ***describe how to prevent injuries***

How can we prevent injuries?

AQA A AQA B EDEXCEL OCR PE OCR G WJEC NICCEA

Being fit does not prevent **illness**, although it is true that a fit person should recover from both illness and injury more quickly than an unfit person. **Injury** is one of the biggest problems that can face a sportsperson. It is often the single most limiting factor relating to performance.

Prevention of injury is better than cure. Injuries are best avoided by:

- **training** correctly and with the aim of developing those factors that are important for the event
- doing sufficient **warm-up** activities, including flexibility and stretching exercises to help prepare the body for work, and warming down
- using **protective equipment**, such as mouth guards, shin pads and helmets which are designed to protect the player, as well as enhance performance
- wearing the **correct clothing** for the sport concerned, as ill-fitting shorts can chafe the inside of the leg and poorly fitting footwear can lead to a host of leg and foot injuries
- playing to the **rules** of the sport. Rules are not just about fair play but were also devised with the safety of the individual in mind. Referees and umpires are duty bound to enforce the rules to help protect players
- checking that the **environment is safe**

Be able to explain how the prevention of injuries can be achieved.

Photo 6.2 Protective clothing for hockey goalkeeper

Injuries caused by violence are common in both contact and non-contact sports. Most occur during contact with:

- an **opponent**, e.g. during a tackle in soccer
- an **implement**, e.g. striking a volley ball incorrectly can cause finger injuries
- the **playing surface**, e.g. playing rugby on frozen ground can be dangerous

Know the main causes of injury.

The treatment of injuries is considered in Chapter 7.

PROGRESS CHECK

1. List four pieces of protective clothing used in four different sports and name the sports they are used in.
2. Explain how contact injuries can occur.

1. e.g. gum shield – rugby; shin pads – soccer; helmet – cycling; kickers – hockey (the list is long). 2. By hitting an opponent, an implement or the playing surface.

6.4 Physical make-up

LEARNING SUMMARY

After studying this section you should be able to:

- ***describe a person's physical make-up***
- ***describe how physical make-up influences performance***

Describing body types

Successful competitors in different sports tend to have different body types. Whilst it is true that not all basketball players are over 2 metres tall, there is no denying the fact that height is important in basketball. It is also true that most sumo wrestlers have a very heavy physique and that female gymnasts tend to be of short stature.

Know what the word 'somatotype' means and be able to describe the three main traits.

The classification of body types is called **somatotyping** and was first introduced by an American called William Sheldon. Sheldon established that there were three main traits in all body types: these he called **endomorph**, **mesomorph** and **ectomorph**. As all people have some of each trait present in their build, each tendency is measured on a scale of 1 to 7.

- A person rating 7 as an endomorph has a large amount of body fat.
- A person rating 7 as a mesomorph is broad shouldered and muscular.
- A person rating 7 as an ectomorph is very tall and thin.

We all have some of each of these body traits in our physical make-up, so our body types are given using a score for each the three traits.

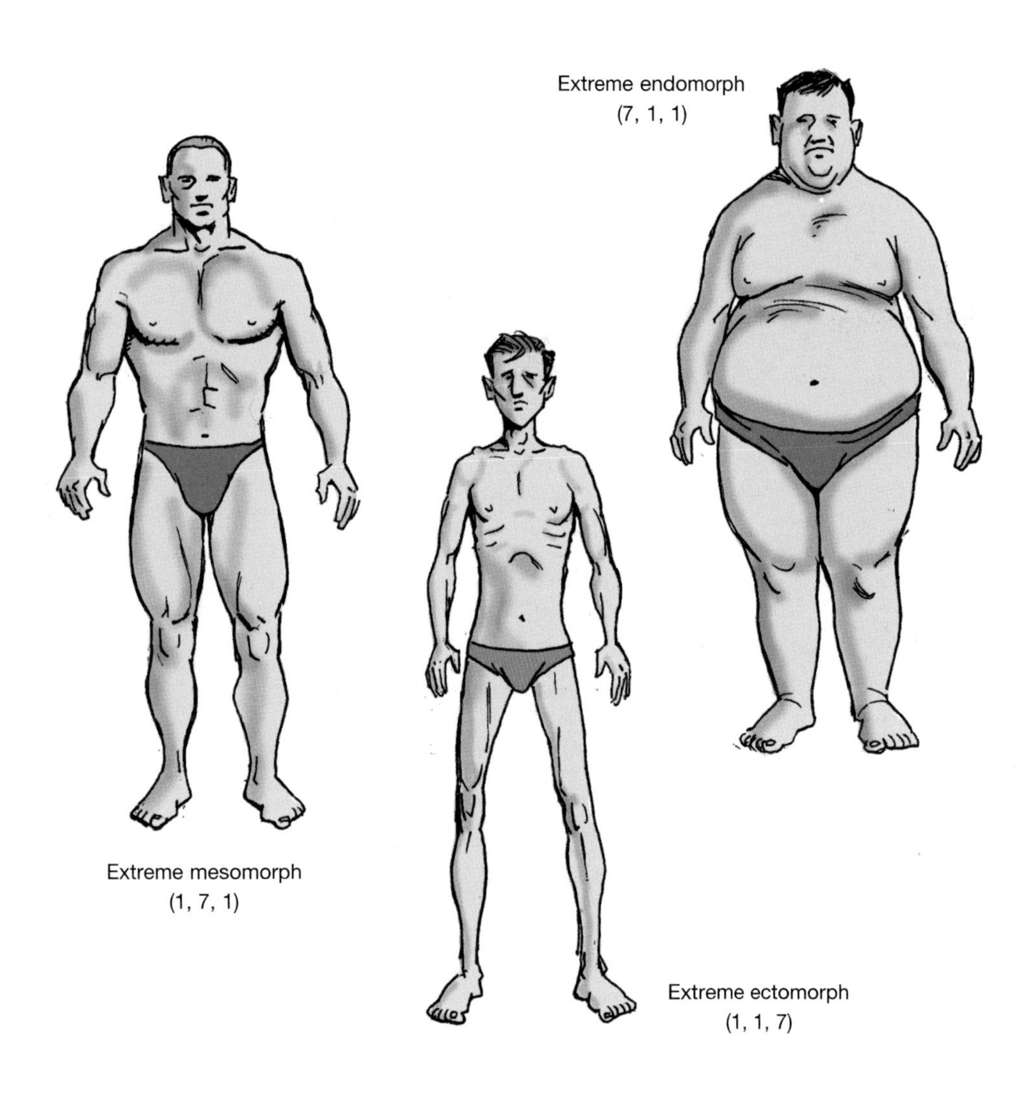

Physical make-up and performance

AQA A AQA B EDEXCEL OCR PE OCR G WJEC NICCEA

The **average** somatotype rating would be 4.4.4 (a bit of everything!) but this is rarely found. Top-level sports players tend to show extremes of one or other of the scales. This can be shown using a somatotype triangle (see Fig 6.3).

Fig 6.3 Somatotype triangle

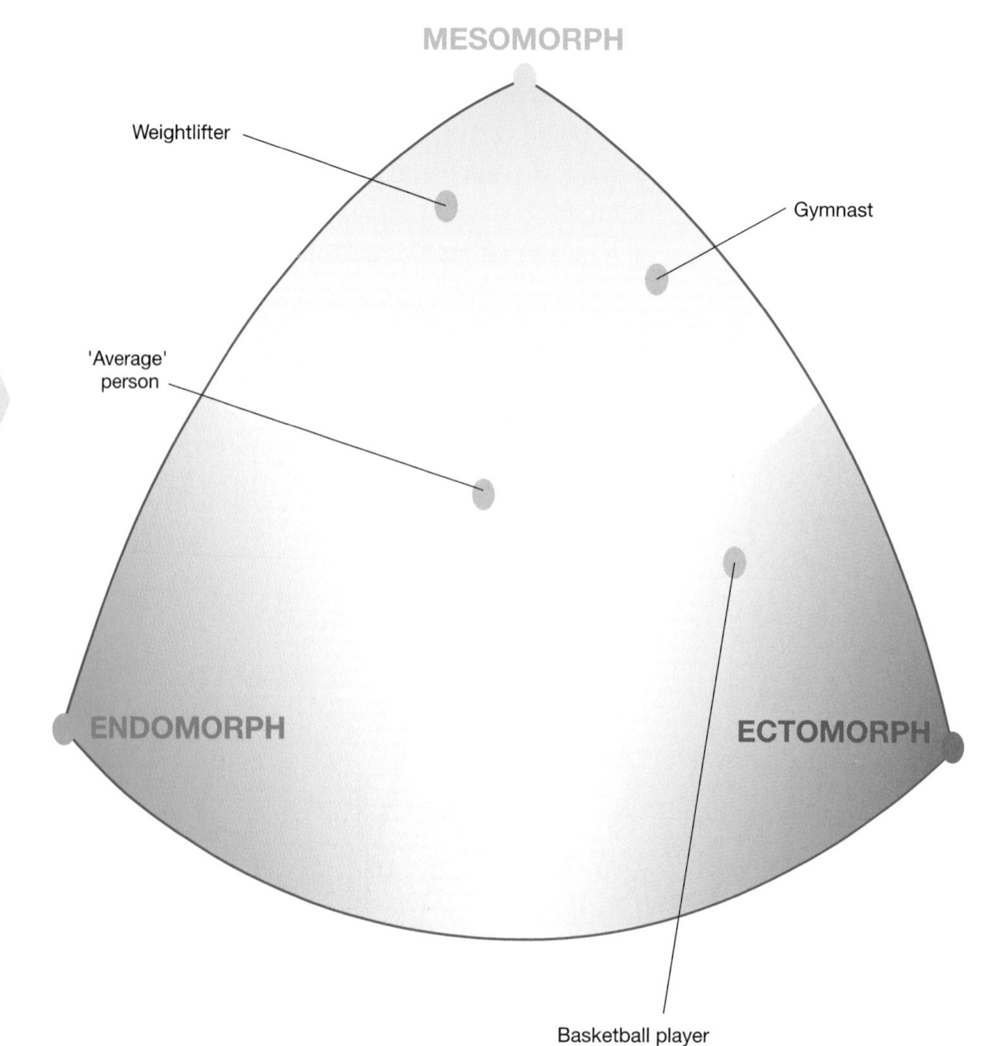

Be able to give examples of sporting activities related to each of the three body types.

In all ratings the:

- first number = endomorph
- second number = mesomorph
- third number = ectomorph

While both men and women can be included in somatotyping, remember that the body shape and size of boys and girls change as they get older. Up to the approximate age of 9 or 10 years boys and girls are very similar in size and build. In adulthood, however, men tend to be larger, stronger and taller than women. Also, women have a smaller ratio of muscle to fat than men. In addition, females experience a monthly menstrual cycle and this can affect a sportswoman's performance. Just prior to menstruation many women have a temporary increase in weight. It would seem that there is an optimum performance time when the female athlete is at her lightest and least stressed (see Fig 6.4).

Fig 6.4 Influence of menstrual cycle on performance

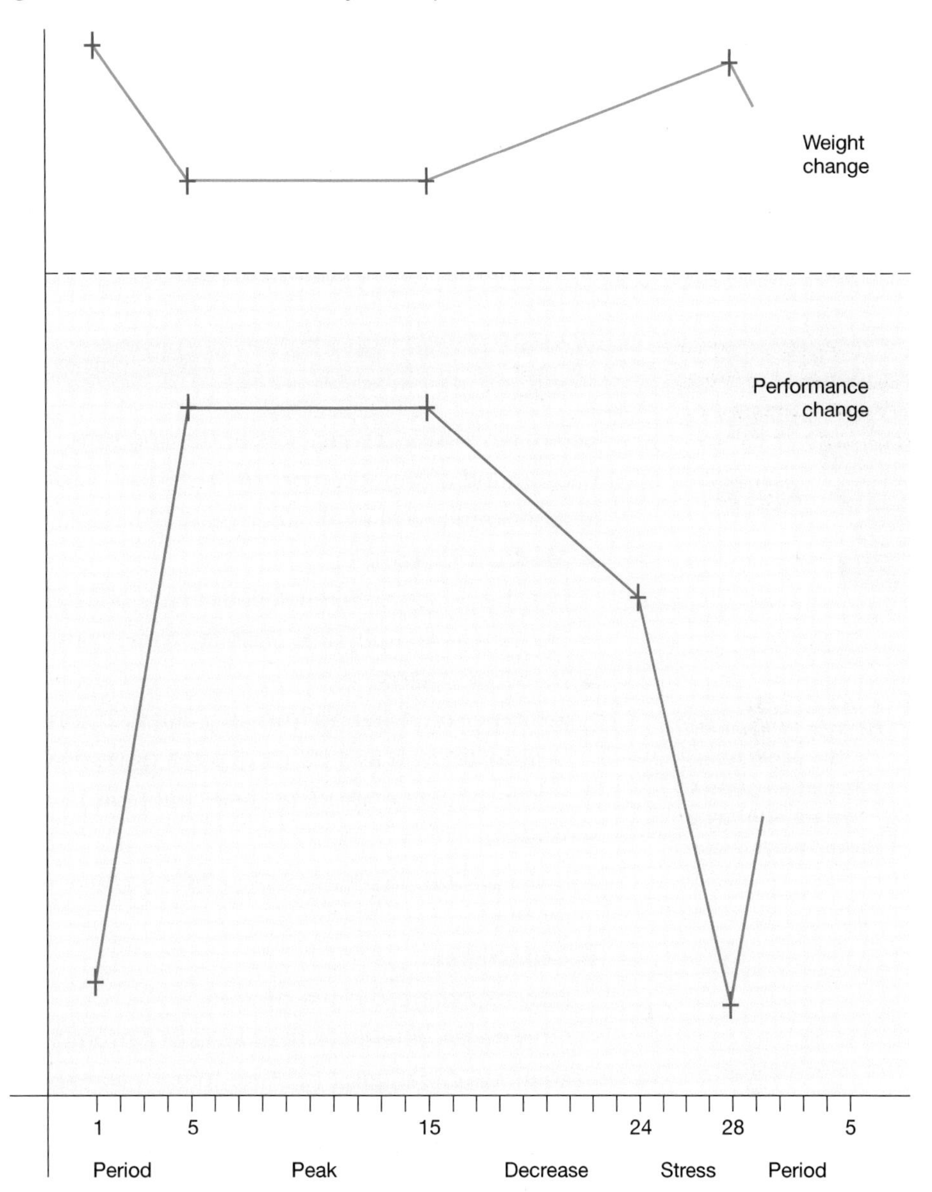

1. Describe the body somatotype that a successful weightlifter might have.
2. Explain why a woman's performance level may vary on a regular basis.
3. What sport would an extreme endomorph be best suited to?

1. A mesomorph: broad shoulders and very muscular. 2. Just prior to menstruation a woman's weight tends to increase and this affects performance levels. 3. Sumo wrestling.

6.5 Personal history

After studying this section you should be able to:

- ***describe how a person's history and status might affect performance***
- ***describe the effect that age might have on performance***

History, status and performance

Before embarking on any sort of training programme it is essential that the background of the sportsperson is studied. Factors that can influence the amount of physical work a person may be able to do are outlined below.

- **Medical history**
  Has the person suffered serious injury or illness in the past?
  Do they have a physical disability to be considered?
- **Medical status**
  Is the person suffering from any illness at this time?
  (Asthmatics can and do carry out a great deal of physical activity, but their coach should be aware of their condition.)
- **Weight**
  Is the person too heavy or too light for their age and if so is there a reason for this?
- **Experience**
  How experienced is the person?
  (This might determine their level of performance. An inexperienced boxer could be in danger if he were to fight an experienced boxer.)

Be able to describe the background information needed before starting a fitness programme.

Age and performance

Age does affect performance in a number of ways.

- **Strength** – full strength is not attained until a person is in their early 20s, and muscular strength can be improved right through a person's 30s.
- **Injury** – older people are more prone to injury than young people. They often take longer to recover from injury.
- **Flexibility** – the very young are very flexible, and this continues with women into their teens. By their 30s men in particular tend to have lost much of their flexibility.
- **Reaction time** – this slows down with age.
- **Experience** – older people tend to make up for their reduced physical capabilities by using their skill levels to better effect. This is known as experience.

1. Why should a person's weight be considered before training starts?
2. How can age be an advantage in some competitions?
3. What is meant by the term 'medical status'?

1. The reason why a person is over or underweight should be established before training starts. 2. Experience comes with age; skill can make up for a lack of strength. 3. Ongoing medical condition (e.g. suffering from asthma).

6.6 Environment

LEARNING SUMMARY

After studying this section you should be able to:

- ***describe the effects that environment might have on performance***

The environment and performance

AQA A | AQA B | EDEXCEL | OCR PE | OCR G | WJEC | NICCEA

KEY POINT **'Training should acclimatise the individual for known competitive conditions.'**

The main factors to be considered are discussed below.

- The **weather** – it can be too hot, cold, humid or windy for a person to produce a high-level performance. Few athletes can produce their best performances when it is raining or very cold. The training programme should reflect the anticipated conditions that will prevail when the competition is due to take place. Remember, it is not just the cold that can affect performance. How many 'fun runners' train in the evenings after work for a special half marathon and then find that the event takes place in the heat of the day?
- The **state of the sports arena** – the track or the sports field can influence performance. Pitches with long or wet grass slow players down. Long grass can also affect the movement of a ball in a game. Artificial surfaces will also affect performance, if the player is used to grass. Inside, a dusty or wet floor in a gymnasium can be slippery and is, therefore, very dangerous.
- The **venue** – the training programme should take into account where the event will be held. This is especially so if the event is to take place at **altitude**. The Mexico Games in 1968 took place 7350 feet (2240 m) above sea level. At this level the air is 25% thinner than at sea level. An athlete's ability to take in and absorb oxygen is much impaired without prior altitude training.

Know the effects and problems of competing at high altitude.

PROGRESS CHECK

1. How can long grass affect performance in soccer?
2. Explain why altitude can affect physical performance.

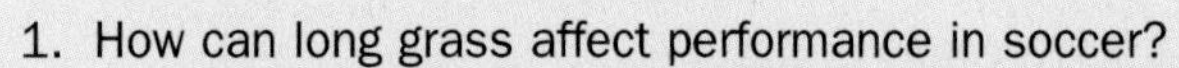

1. Ball will roll more slowly. Player will run more slowly and find it difficult to turn quickly. 2. As the air is thinner, it makes it more difficult to take in and absorb oxygen.

6.7 Drug use and abuse

After studying this section you should be able to:

- *describe the main drugs used in sport*
- *describe the effects of drug abuse*

Use of drugs in sport

AQA A AQA B EDEXCEL OCR PE OCR G WJEC NICCEA

Many different types of drug feature in sport. Some are used and some are abused.

The **use** of some drugs is quite acceptable in sport: asthmatics and hay fever sufferers are allowed to take approved drugs for example. The use of some prescribed drugs to overcome illness is also acceptable. However, the **abuse** or **misuse** of drugs to enhance performance is considered unacceptable.

Effects of drug abuse in sport

AQA A AQA B EDEXCEL OCR PE OCR G WJEC NICCEA

It is easy to remember the drugs that you have to know about. They do not come at Christmas but at **CASHMAS**!

- **cannabis** – a relaxant
- **analgesics** – pain killers
- **solvents** – intoxicants
- **hallucinogens** – distort perception
- **miscellaneous** – include anabolic steroids, opiates, laxatives and diuretics
- **antidepressants** – relieve anxiety
- **stimulants** – improve reaction

Not all of these drugs are banned by the International Olympic Committee (IOC) but from 1967 onwards an increasing number have been banned. At the last count over 4000 types and variants of drug had been outlawed for use in sport. Table 6.5 shows the main classes of banned drug and also describes their effects. You can see why people have used these drugs in the past and why modern athletes may be tempted to use them even though they are banned.

Table 6.5 Banned drugs and their effects

Banned drug	Effect
beta-blockers	helps to give a steady hand, such as is needed in shooting and archery
analgesics	decreases the amount of pain from injury; can increase the pain threshold during competition
diuretics	removes fluids by excessive urination to bring about weight loss; also act as a masking agent for other substances
stimulants	increases alertness; reduces fatigue; increases competitiveness and aggression
anabolic steroids	increases muscle size and thus strength; aids recovery from physical stress and injury; produces a more competitive and aggressive nature
polypeptide hormones	similar effects to anabolic steroids

BAD SAP will help you to remember the groups.

Have a sound knowledge of the banned groups of drugs and their effects.

Many people see the use of these banned drugs as a form of **cheating** because they enhance a person's natural performance. This is seen as being morally wrong. However, these drugs are also banned because of the dangerous side effects that they can have on the sportsperson (see Table 6.6).

KEY POINT

Many drugs are banned to protect the performer.

Have a sound knowledge of the negative side effects that these drugs might have.

Table 6.6 Banned drugs and their side effects

Banned drug	Dangerous side effect
beta-blockers	as they act by lowering the heart rate they can cause circulation problems; also physically and psychologically addictive
analgesics	low blood pressure; heart and liver problems
diuretics	cramps and dehydration
stimulants	high blood pressure; heart and liver problems
anabolic steroids	high blood pressure; heart disease; infertility; cancer; women often grow facial hair, become flat-chested and their voices grow deeper; men often find that their testicles disappear into their bodies
polypeptide hormones	strokes and abnormal growths

Blood doping

Blood doping does not involve the abuse of drugs but it is banned for similar reasons.

Blood doping is the practice of taking blood from a sportsperson, separating out the red blood cells and keeping them for use at a later date. The body replaces any blood removed from it in a short space of time. However, just before a race, the sportsperson will put back the retained red cells, thus giving a very high red cell count.

Red cells carry oxygen to the muscles. A very high cell count means that the muscles get extra oxygen and can work harder for longer periods of time. This method of enhancing performance is attractive to people involved in long distance events, such as the marathon.

Note the dangers in blood doping.

The negative side effects of blood doping are that allergic reactions can develop, kidneys can be damaged and capillaries can become permanently blocked.

EPO (Erythropoietin) is something of a newcomer to the drug scene, having arrived in the late 1990s. It should be classed as a polypeptide hormone as it is an artificially produced hormone, but it has a similar effect to blood doping.

1. What is drug abuse in the context of sport?
2. Name four banned drugs.

1. It is the misuse of drugs to enhance performance. 2. Four from beta-blockers, analgesics, diuretics, stimulants, anabolic steroids, polypeptide hormones.

Sample GCSE questions

Explain how age can be a factor which influences participation in physical recreation and sport.

As people get older their bodies deteriorate and so become less efficient. They tend to participate less. They change to less demanding activities such as bowls. The bodies of young people are not fully developed, so some sports are unsuitable. However, sports like gymnastics are best suited to the young.

Remember 'age' means both old and young.

[2]

Body type is a factor that can determine potential performance in sport.

(a) Describe the characteristics of an extreme ectomorph.

linear in shape, thin, narrow shoulders and hips, has little muscle or fat

Shape, hip and shoulder size are important.

[2]

(b) Select a sport or event in which those with ectomorphic tendencies may excel.

high jump, long distance running, basketball

Any one of these is suitable.

[1]

NICCEA Q29 1998 Q14 1999

Which **two** socially acceptable drugs are legal, despite the possible health risks to those taking them?

alcohol, smoking or tobacco

[2]

State **two** physical dangers athletes may face if they take anabolic steroids.

kidney/liver damage, male characteristics in females, heart disease, cancer, high blood pressure, infertility

Give any TWO of these, not all of them.

[2]

State **two** reasons why an athlete might take anabolic steroids despite the risks.

to increase training potential, to win, gain wealth, increase aggression, improve power, improve strength, enhance performance

There is a wide range of possible answers but choose only two.

[2]

EDEXCEL 1999 Paper 1 Q34

Exam practice questions

(a) List the **four** food groups that do not provide energy.

....

.... **[4]**

(b) Which food groups would provide the main source of energy for the following events?

(i) 1000 metre sprint ....

(ii) 5 minutes jogging ....

(iii) 3 hours cycling ....

(iv) running a marathon .... **[4]**

(c) Which body somatotype would be best suited to the following activities?

(i) 100 metre sprint ....

(ii) long distance running ....

(iii) sumo wrestling..

(iv) rowing .... **[4]**

EDEXCEL 1999 Paper 1 Q32 & 33

Chapter

Sports-related injuries

The following topics are covered in this chapter:

- ***Safe practice***
- ***Soft tissue injuries and their treatment***
- ***Hard tissue injuries***
- ***Miscellaneous injuries and illnesses***
- ***Sports injuries and first aid***
- ***Specific sports injuries***

7.1 Safe practice

After studying this section you should be able to:

- ***explain how to avoid injuries***
- ***understand the Health and Safety at Work Act with regard to sport***

How to avoid injuries

Injuries (and the after effects of injuries) are perhaps the single most limiting factor to physical performance.

There are **six** main criteria for avoiding sports injuries.

1. **Correct training** – make sure that you have practised the skills for the sport, you are fit for the sport and that you are playing the sport at a level you can cope with.
2. **Warm up and warm down** – before you start any sport make sure that you have warmed up correctly, so that your body is ready for the rough and tumble of the sport. At the end, do not forget to cool down.
3. **Use protective equipment** – some sports insist that you protect yourself. Remember that you cannot play a game of soccer without wearing shin pads. Protection is essential in games such as cricket and for goalkeepers in hockey.
4. **Wear appropriate clothing** – make sure that you are wearing the right kit for the sport and that it is in good working order. Do not wear jewellery, watches or earrings which can be a real hazard.
5. **Understand and abide by the rules** – know and play to the rules. They were developed to protect you, as well as to test your skill and abilities. Listen to coaches and referees: they should know the rules and how to interpret them.
6. **Environmental hazards** – always check that the playing area is safe. Too often hazardous litter is scattered over a pitch; damp or dusty indoor floor surfaces can also be dangerous. Do not forget frost, rain and wind when playing outdoors. These conditions can affect pitches. If the environment proves hazardous enforce a postponement.

These aspects are often asked for in examinations.

The Health and Safety at Work Act 1974

AQA A AQA B EDEXCEL OCR PE OCR G WJEC

Schools, sports centres, leisure centres and stadia all have a **duty of care** to the sports performer. This Act insists that whoever puts on a sporting activity should put the **safety of the performer first and foremost**.

Know the seven main features of the Act.

They must make sure that:

- all equipment is safe to use
- the group size is appropriate to the activity
- the ability of the group matches the event
- activities and training sessions are properly planned and controlled
- safety equipment is available and in good working order
- first aid is available
- procedures for calling the emergency services are in place

PROGRESS CHECK

1. What should always be worn while playing sport?
2. What should never be worn while playing sport?
3. What are the seven features of the Health and Safety at Work Act 1974?

1. The correct clothes for the sport in question. 2. Jewellery, watches and especially earrings. 3. Safe equipment, appropriate group size, activities are suitable for ability, activities are planned and controlled, safety equipment available and working, first aid is available, procedures for calling emergency services in place.

7.2 Soft tissue injuries

LEARNING SUMMARY

After studying this section you should be able to:

- *describe a soft tissue injury*
- *describe open wounds and closed wounds, and their treatment*

What is a soft tissue injury?

AQA A AQA B EDEXCEL OCR PE OCR G WJEC

These are injuries to any part of the body except bone. They account for over 90% of all sports injuries.

Open and closed wounds and their treatment

AQA A AQA B EDEXCEL OCR PE OCR G WJEC

There are two main types of soft tissue injuries: **open wounds** and **closed wounds**.

Know the difference between open and closed wounds.

KEY POINT

Open wounds are those that allow blood to escape (see Table 7.1).

Table 7.1 Open wounds

Type of open wound	Causes	Treatment
cuts and grazes	contact with hard objects and surfaces	application of pressure, raising the affected area
blisters	repeated rubbing of skin	clean and apply antiseptic, cover with sterile dressing
chafing	ill-fitting clothing	remove source of irritation, apply antiseptic cream

KEY POINT

Closed wounds are those where there is no external bleeding (see Table 7.2).

Remember that bleeding may occur under the skin. This is a bruise.

Table 7.2 Closed wounds

Type of closed wound	Causes	Symptoms	Treatment
bruising	impact with hard object	pain, swelling, discolouration	RICE
strained muscles	stretching of 'cold' muscles	pain, tenderness	RICE
torn muscles	poor warm-up, over-stretching, sudden movement	sharp pain, discolouration	RICE, medical advice
tendonitis	repeated stress of tendon	pain, swelling, inflammation	rest, followed by slow, gentle exercise
sprained ligament	sudden forcing of joint beyond normal range	pain, swelling, loss of movement	RICE
meniscal tears*	violent impact, sudden twisting	pain, loss of movement	surgical repair

*Meniscal cartilage is wedge-shaped and found in mobile joints such as the knee (see Chapter 1).

You should know how to treat open and closed wounds.

KEY POINT

RICE stands for:
Rest
Ice
Compression
Elevation (see page 100–101)

PROGRESS CHECK

1. Explain how blisters are caused and what treatment to recommend.
2. What are the main symptoms of bruising?
3. What type of tissue is damaged in a 'meniscal tear'? Where could it occur?

1. By the repeated rubbing of skin; area should be cleaned, antiseptic applied and the area should be covered with sterile dressing. 2. Pain, swelling and discolouration. 3. Cartilage found in mobile joints such as the knee.

7.3 Hard tissue injuries

LEARNING SUMMARY

After studying this section you should be able to:

- ***describe the main causes of hard tissue injuries***
- ***describe the main types of fracture and their symptoms***

Causes of fractures

AQA A AQA B EDEXCEL OCR PE OCR G WJEC

Know the difference between hard and soft tissue injuries.

Hard tissue injuries are injuries to **bone** tissue and, fortunately for the sportsperson, occur far less frequently than soft tissue injuries. A hard tissue injury is also called a **fracture**.

Fractures are most common in contact sports and are usually caused by:

- contact with an **opponent** – as in a tackle
- contact with an **implement** – as when a hard ball hits the hand
- contact with the **playing surface** – as when falling on frozen ground

Types of fractures and their symptoms

AQA A AQA B EDEXCEL OCR PE OCR G WJEC

There are four main types of fracture.

1. **Closed** fracture – this is when the bone is broken but the skin is intact.
2. **Open** fracture – this is when the end of the broken bone appears through the surface of the skin.
3. **Compound** fracture – this is when the broken bone has caused another injury.
4. **Stress** fracture – this is when cracks appear along the length of a bone as a result of repeated stress on the bone over a long period of time.

The general symptoms of the first three types of fracture are:

- the break of the bone may be felt or heard
- pain and tenderness
- swelling and a possible abnormal shape in the painful area

Symptoms of stress fractures may occur more gradually. In long distance runners they are often called **shin soreness** or **shin splints**.

KEY POINT

Treatment of all types of fracture should be provided by a medical expert (see Fig 7.1).

Fig 7.1 Types of fracture

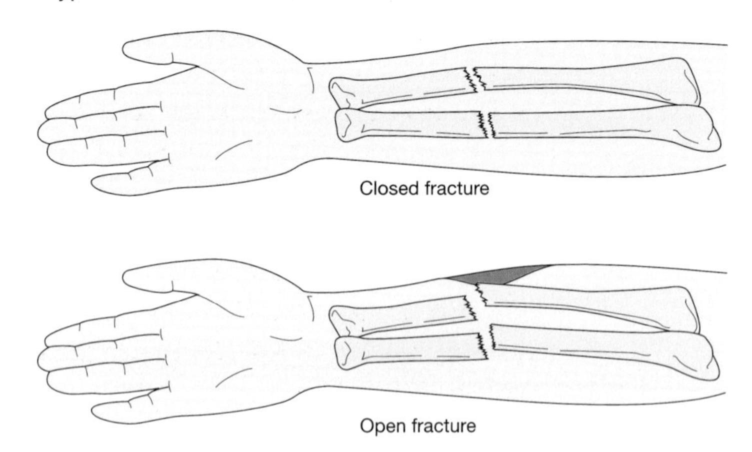

Both closed and open fractures may be complicated by injury to blood vessels, nerves or adjacent organs caused by fractured bone ends or fragments of bone.

1. What are the three most common causes of a fracture?
2. Explain the term 'compound fracture'.
3. What are shin splints?

1. Contact with an opponent, an implement or hard (frozen) ground. 2. This is when a broken bone has caused other injuries. 3. Cracks that appear along the length of the bone.

7.4 Miscellaneous injuries and illnesses

After studying this section you should be able to:

- ***describe a range of common conditions that might affect the sportsperson***

Some common conditions

- **Winding** is caused by a blow to the concentration of nerves in the upper abdomen called the **solar plexus**. This causes the diaphragm to go into spasm. Clothing should be loosened, the sufferer should sit in a relaxed position and take deep breaths.
- **Hypothermia** is the lowering of the body temperature below 35°C. When this happens the nervous system is affected, muscular rigidity can develop and the heart beats irregularly. Unconsciousness may follow. Treatment is to bring the body temperature back to normal (36/37°C) in a steady and sustained manner. Hypothermia may occur in canoeing and hill walking.
- **Hyperthermia** is often referred to as **heat exhaustion**. This is when the body temperature rises above normal, owing to excessive effort and dehydration. Loss of co-ordination and shock may develop. Treatment is to place the individual in a cool place, provide liquids and seek medical help. Hyperthermia may occur during long distance running.

Know what may cause hypothermia and hyperthermia.

- **Stitch** is a pain in the side of the abdomen or in the lower chest brought on by physical activity. It is best described as a form of cramp of the diaphragm and it restricts deep breathing. The recommended treatment is to breathe in deeply and out shallowly, and to keep bending and straightening.
- **Cramp** is an instantaneous contraction of a skeletal muscle that cannot be relaxed. It can last for a few seconds or several minutes. Its precise cause is unknown as muscle cramps can occur during hard physical exercise or during complete relaxation. Causes are thought to be a lack of salt or minerals in the diet, or a temporary restriction of blood to the affected muscle. The recommended treatment is to stretch the affected muscle manually and then massage it (see Fig 7.2).

You should know what the causes and treatment are for cramp, winding and stitch.

Fig 7.2 Treatment for cramp

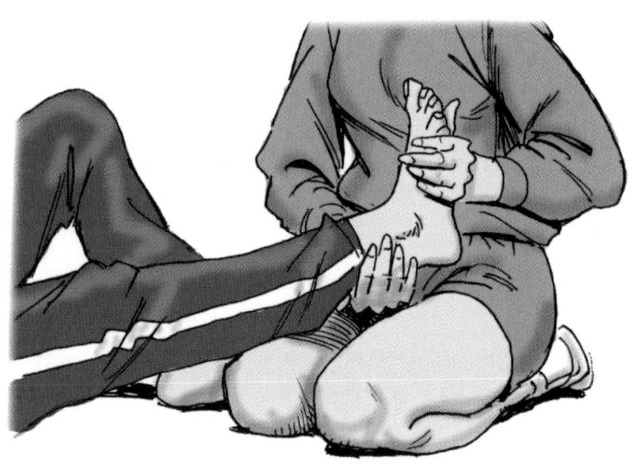

For cramp in calf muscles

For cramp in thigh muscles

- **Shock** is caused by insufficient blood circulating round the body, often owing to severe bleeding and/or severe pain. It shows itself in a number of ways: clammy skin, shallow and rapid breathing, a feeling of dizziness coupled with a desire to vomit and possibly with a lapse into unconsciousness. The recommended treatment is to arrest any bleeding, place the sufferer in the recovery position, provide reassurance and seek medical help (see Fig 7.3).

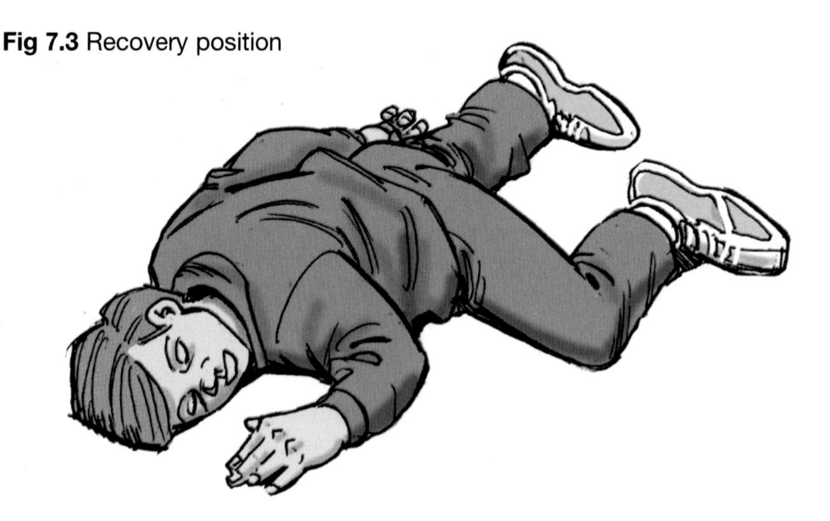

Fig 7.3 Recovery position

1. What is normal body temperature?
2. What is another name for hyperthermia?
3. Describe a cramp. How long can it last?

1. 36 or 37°C. 2. Heat exhaustion. 3. Instantaneous contraction of skeletal muscle that cannot be relaxed; lasts from a few seconds to several minutes.

7.5 Sports injuries and first aid

After studying this section you should be able to:

- ***explain what to do in the event of any injury***

What to do if someone gets hurt

AQA A · AQA B · EDEXCEL · OCR PE · OCR G · WJEC

Should an injury occur it is advisable to:

- **stop** the game or activity at once
- **look** at the affected area
- **listen** to the injured person (can they tell you what the problem is?)
- **feel** very gently round the affected area to detect any abnormality
- **apply** first aid treatment if you know what you are doing

Soft tissue injuries

You should be able to describe what to do if confronted with a minor injury.

For soft tissue injuries when the casualty is conscious, the treatment usually follows the **RICE** formula (see Fig 7.4).

- **R**est the injured part of the body at once.
- **I**ce should be applied to the affected part. This can reduce swelling and muscle spasm. It will restrict the flow of blood to the injured area.

- **C**ompress the injured area by means of an elastic bandage. This also helps to prevent swelling. Note that the bandage should not be so tight as to completely restrict the flow of blood.
- **E**levate the injured part. This should only be attempted if the movement does not cause pain.

Fig 7.4 The RICE formula

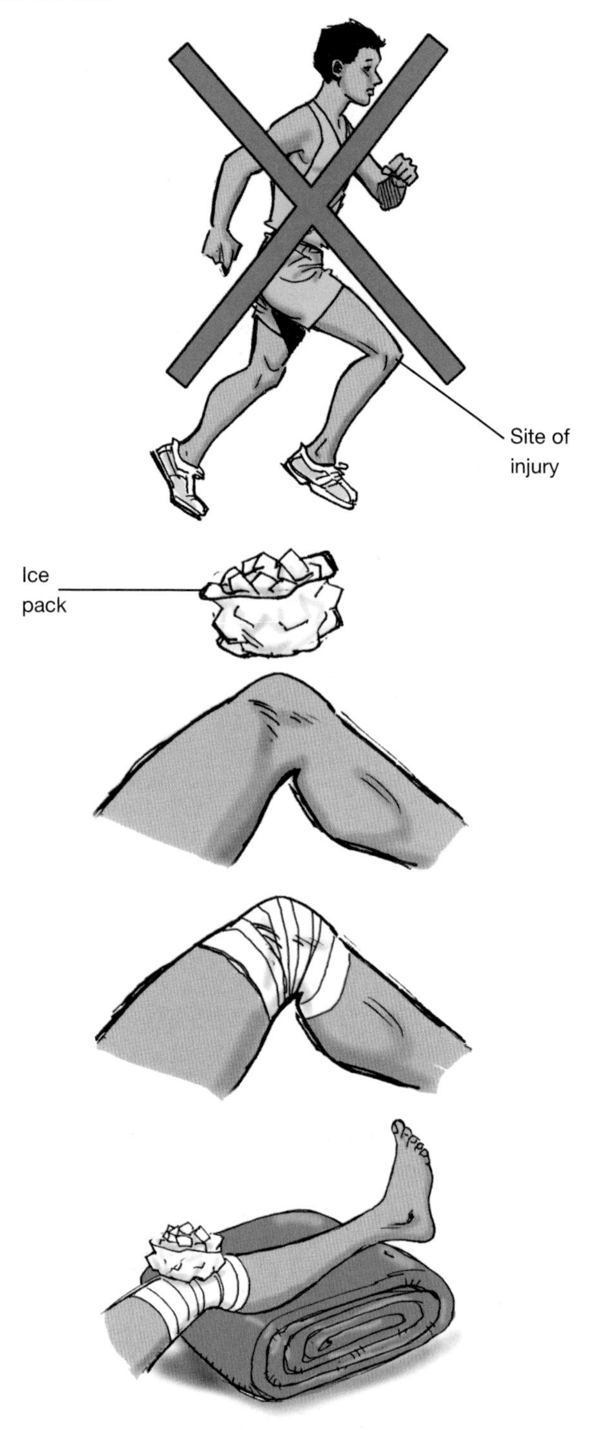

What to do if there is no breathing or pulse

Remember that the RICE formula is for **minor injuries** only. Should a more **serious** accident occur, then the **DRABC** routine should be followed.

- **DANGER** – check that both you and the casualty are not in any further danger while treatment is carried out. Clear the surrounding area.

You should be able to explain both the RICE formula and DRABC routine and be able to apply them to the appropriate situations.

- **RESPONSE** – try to get some reply from the injured person. This will indicate whether they are conscious. Take care if you are shaking the casualty: you do not want to cause further injury.
- **AIRWAY** – check to see if the airway is open. If not, clear any obstruction such as false teeth, a mouth guard or vomit. Gently tilt the head backwards, as this will clear the tongue from the air passage. If there is still no sign of breathing then mouth-to-mouth ventilation may be required.
- **BREATHING** – if the casualty cannot breathe for himself or herself, then you will have to do it for them. You do this by blowing your air into the casualty's mouth. However, continued mouth-to-mouth ventilation is pointless if there is no blood circulation.
- **CIRCULATION** – circulation of the blood is essential. The best way to check for this is to see if you can find a pulse at the carotid artery in the neck. If there is no pulse then external compression (cardiac massage) may help the heart to start working again (see Fig 7.5).

Do not try cardiac massage unless you have had proper training.

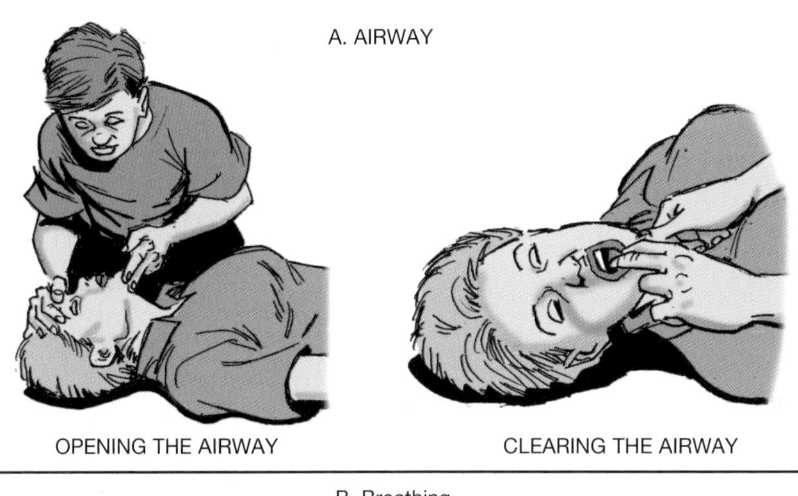

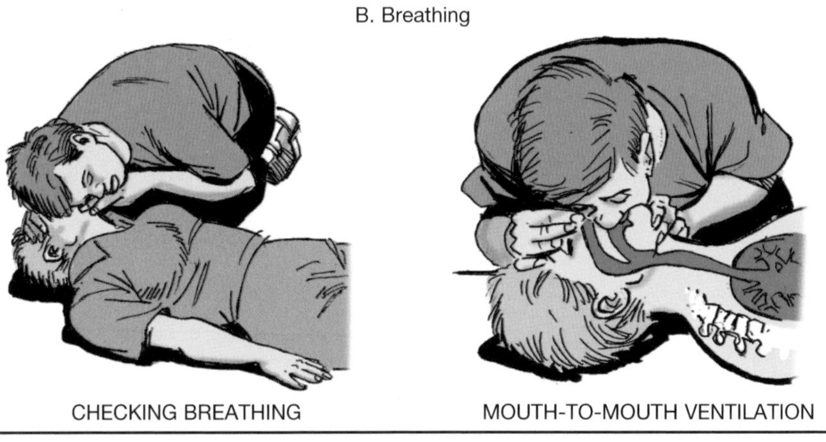

C. CIRCULATION

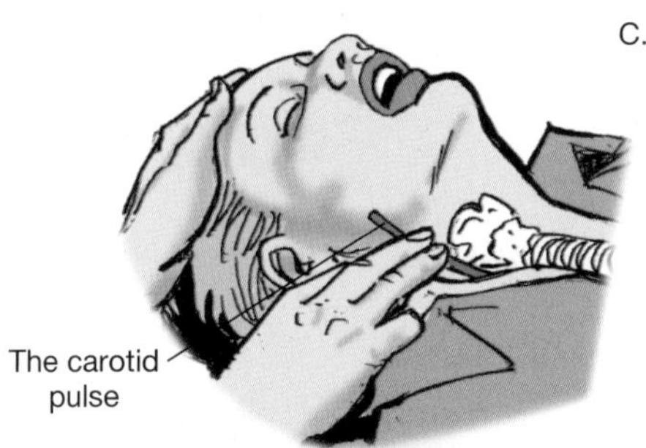

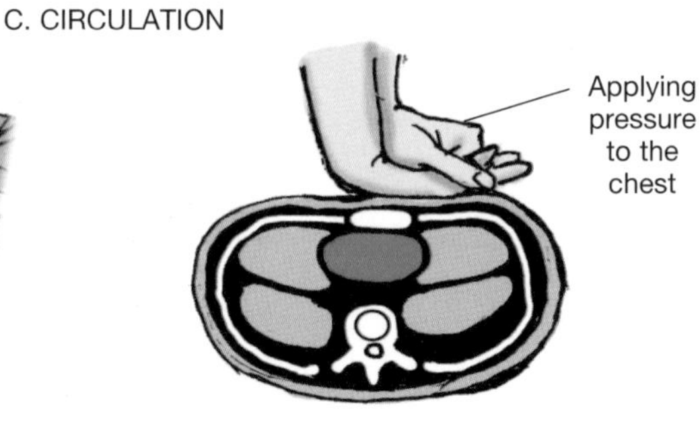

Fig 7.5 The ABC of First Aid

Do not attempt to move the casualty in any way if there is the least sign of any other injury. Just make sure that the airway is kept open.

If the casualty remains unconscious but is breathing, seek medical advice. The safest position to put them in while you arrange this is the **recovery position**. In this position the airway will be kept open and the casualty will not be able to roll over (see Fig 7.3, page 100).

1. In the event of an accident or injury, what are the first three things you should do?
2. Explain the RICE formula.
3. What do the letters DRABC stand for?

1. Stop, Look, Listen. 2. Rest, Ice, Compression, Elevation. 3. Danger, Response, Airway, Breathing, Circulation.

7.6 Specific sports injuries

After studying this section you should be able to:

- ***describe the injuries that are common to some sports***

Injuries reflect the nature of the game

Many injuries are closely associated with certain sports, particularly body contact sports such as rugby. Some injuries will reflect the position a person plays in within a team. In football, the goalkeeper often sustains different types of injuries to a striker. Participants in recreational activities, such as aerobics and keep fit, can still get injuries, but of a different type to those of the games player (see Fig 7.6).

Fig 7.6 Injuries associated with specific sports

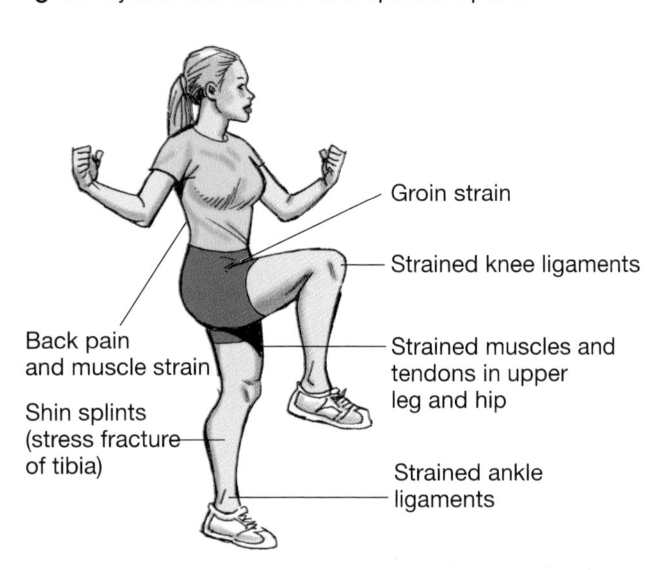

Fig 7.6 Injuries associated with specific sports *(continued)*

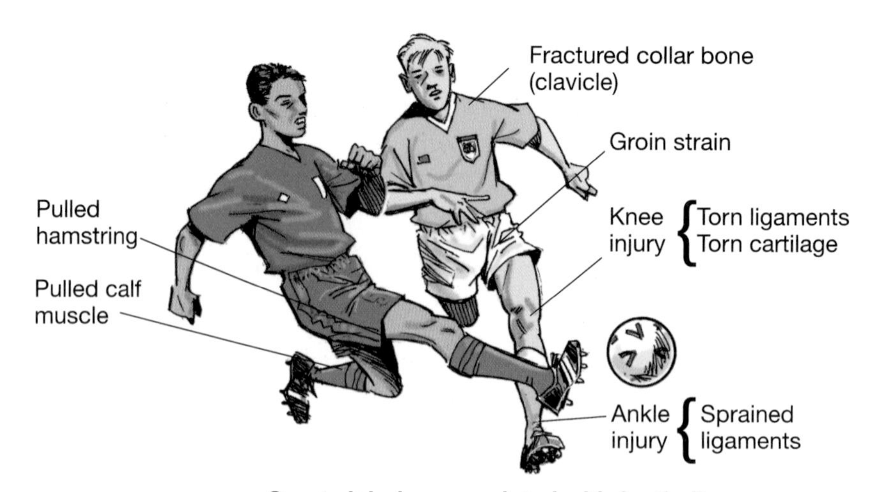

Sports injuries associated with football

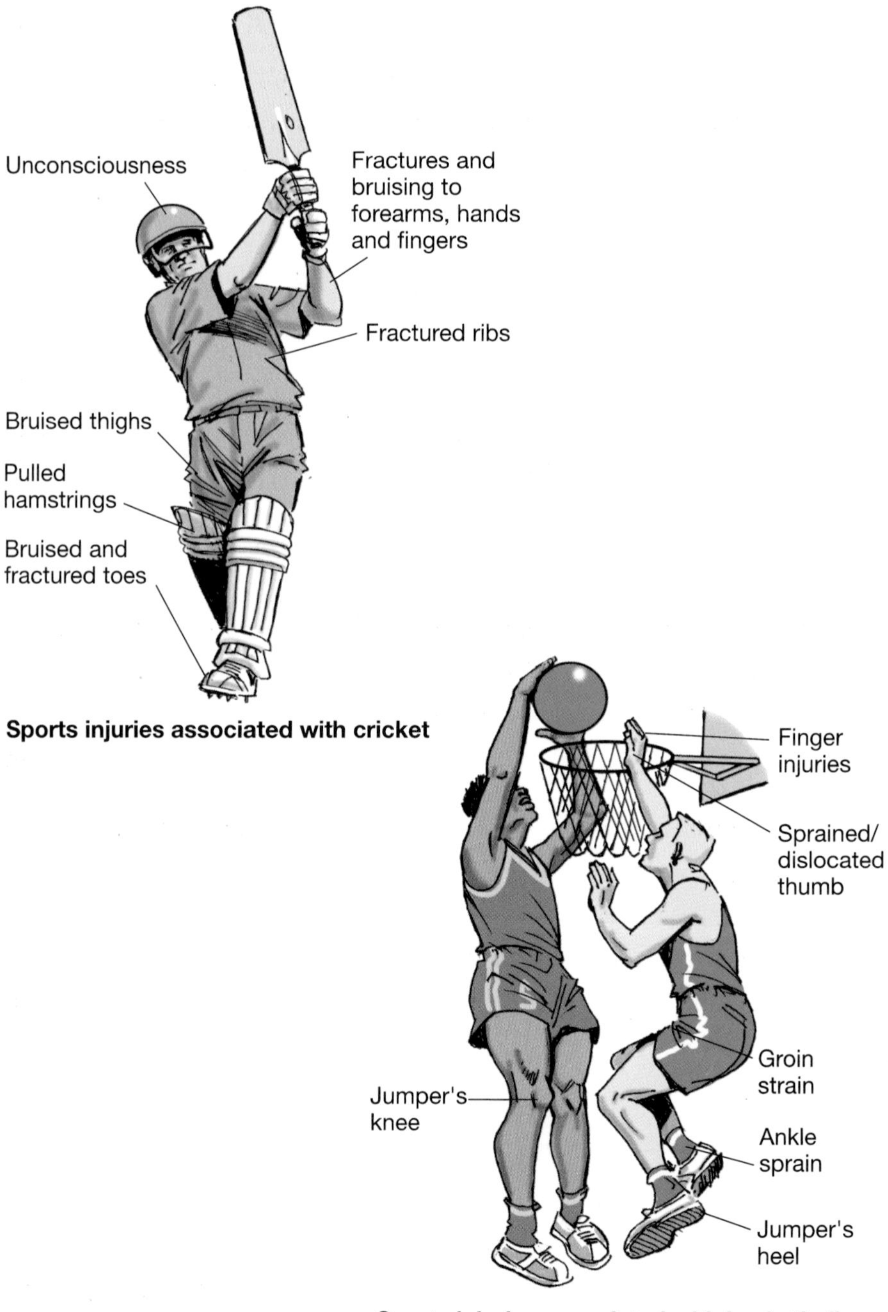

Sports injuries associated with cricket

Sports injuries associated with basketball

Sample GCSE questions

1. Name and describe **two** different soft tissue injuries that might occur as a result of taking part in physical activity.

   Muscle strain or pull: a tear in a muscle or damaged fibre in a muscle owing to over stretching.
   Graze: skin is scraped off the body when performer falls on hard ground or on an artificial surface.
   Cut: the skin is damaged and blood flows from the wound. Sharp materials such as studs can cause this.
   Bruise: often caused by a blow or a kick to the muscle. Blood leaks from damaged capillaries but stays inside the skin. Swelling and discolouration may be evident.

   Only TWO of these possible answers are needed. A complete answer is required in each case to get full marks.

   [4]

2. State **four** factors that are part of the Health and Safety at Work Act 1974 which are concerned with safety in Physical Education.

   All equipment is safe to use; the group size is appropriate to the activity; the ability of the group matches the event; activities and training sessions are properly planned and controlled; safety equipment is available and in good working order; first aid is available; procedures for calling in the emergency services are in place.

   Only FOUR of these are asked for, but know the rest.

   [4]

OCR 1999/2000

3. (i) What is a sprained ligament?

   torn ligament tissue around a joint, often caused by a twist or wrench

   [1]

   (ii) State **two** ways in which you could help relieve the pain for someone with a sprained ligament.

   any two from Rest, Ice, Compression, Elevation

   [2]

   (iii) Give **two** reasons why jewellery should be removed when taking part in sport.

   any two from can catch on equipment; can cut/hurt self or opponent; can distract performer; can get tangled and cause choking

   [2]

OCR 1999 Paper 1 QB2 & 2000 Paper 1 QB2

Exam practice questions

Simon was watching a hockey match when one of the players slipped, fell over and injured their ankle.

(a) Apart from a sprain, what type of injury might they also have sustained?

.... **[1]**

(b) If it was a sprain, what treatment should be given to them?

....

....

....

.... **[4]**

After the match, Simon went back to the car park and found the umpire apparently unconscious by his car. Fortunately, Simon was a first aider.

(c) What **five** steps should he follow?

....

....

....

....

.... **[5]**

(d) If Simon found the umpire had no pulse, what should his next action be?

....

.... **[1]**

EDEXCEL 1998 Paper 1 Q38

Chapter 8 Sport within society

The following topics are covered in this chapter:

- ***Leisure***
- ***Reasons for participation***
- ***Factors affecting an individual's participation***

8.1 Leisure, recreation and sport

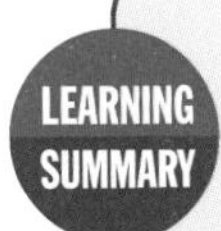

After completing this section you should be able to:

- ***explain leisure***
- ***explain the increase in our leisure time***

What is leisure?

AQA A AQA B EDEXCEL OCR PE OCR G WJEC NICCEA

We all have certain obligations, duties and needs. After these have been met, we often have some time left when we can do just as we want: we have a **freedom of choice**. This time to spend as we please is called **leisure time** (see Fig 8.1).

Fig 8.1 The leisure time continuum

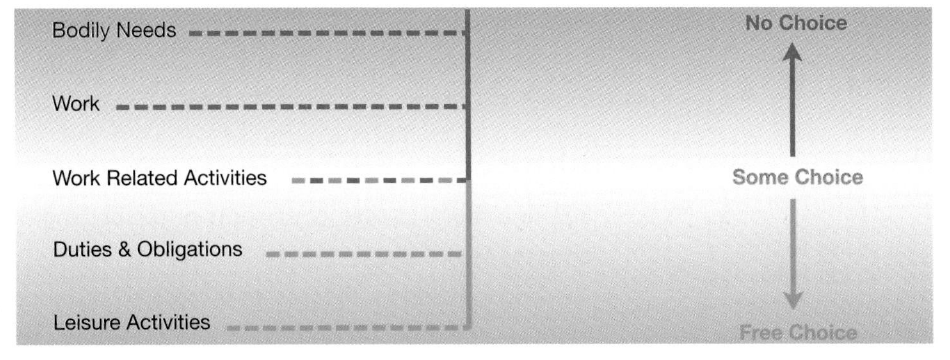

Leisure time can be described as 'that time not needed to meet our social and bodily needs'.

In this definition, our bodily needs include eating and sleeping, and our social needs include work or school, duty and obligations.

What people do in their leisure time varies. Many people spend their leisure time taking part in **recreational activities**. Recreation tends to be planned and may include physical activities.

Recreational activities can be defined as 'those activities that we choose to follow for their own sake'.

People involve themselves in **physical recreation** for a number of reasons.

- **Physical benefits** – they help you to become fit and healthy.
- **Mental benefits** – they relieve stress and tension, are fun to do and make you feel better in yourself.
- **Social benefits** – they help you to meet people, make new friends and develop social skills, such as consideration and appreciation of the needs of others.

Rules are needed in both physical recreation and sport for our safety, as well as to make the game fair.

Recreational activities often have **rules**. Following the rules is sometimes of less importance than the fun of participation and they may not be adhered to fully. However, some rules are important for safety, whether we are playing for fun or competitively. When the rules take on a major significance, and the competitive element of the activity becomes more important, then the recreational activity is referred to as a **sport**.

Be able to distinguish between leisure, recreation and sport.

A sport may be defined as 'an activity requiring physical prowess or skill together with some hierarchical element and which results in a winner'.

Increases in our leisure time

AQA A | AQA B | EDEXCEL | OCR PE | OCR G | WJEC | NICCEA

People are getting more and more leisure time. This is owing to various changes in our lives.

- **Working life** – the average adult's working life is now much shorter than it was 100 years ago. People do not start work until at least 16 years of age, sometimes 21 or later if they go to university, and retirement age is currently 60 for women and 65 for men. In some jobs retirement can come as early as 55. Better health care means that people live longer. A hundred years ago school for many ended at 11 years of age. Retirement was limited and few people retired with a pension.
- **Working week** – this has also reduced over the last 100 years. Compared with the 45 or 50 hours worked per week 100 years ago, many full-time jobs today are for only 35 hours a week, often spread over a 5-day week. In addition many people work shifts or restrict themselves to part-time employment.

You should be able to explain what has contributed to the increase in leisure time.

- **Unemployment** – there is an increasing number of people who do not work at all. Some are unfortunate in that they cannot find a job, others choose not to work, relying on a partner to support them. Many mothers and some fathers find that work is not an option if they have to look after very young children.
- **Holiday time** – this has increased over the last 100 years, together with the advent of paid holiday time. Legislation giving all workers paid holiday time came into effect in 1938 and today many people have paid holiday time of up to 5 weeks, including bank holidays.
- **Labour-saving devices** – these have become very popular and are now more efficient and affordable. Most homes have microwave cookers, washing machines, dishwashers and tumble dryers. These have all helped to reduce the time spent on duties and obligations.

1. Give definitions for 'leisure time' and 'sport'.
2. List three benefits that people might get from physical recreation.
3. List four reasons why adults might not have a job.
4. When were laws first passed to ensure that all workers got paid holidays?

1. Leisure time: that time not needed to meet our social and bodily needs. Sport: an activity requiring physical prowess or skill, together with some element of competition. 2. Physical benefits, mental benefits, social benefits. 3. They might be retired, unemployed, a house parent or have chosen not to work. 4. 1938

8.2 Reasons for participation

After completing this section you should be able to:

- ***explain why people take part in sport***
- ***explain how sports participation has grown***

Why people take part in sport

AQA A AQA B EDEXCEL

Know the four main reasons why people take part in sport.

Most people who elect to play sport during their leisure time do so for a variety of reasons.

1. Sport is **enjoyable**. It helps people to look good and feel good, and can give a sense of achievement. It can also stimulate aesthetic awareness.
2. Sport contributes to **good health** and aids **recovery from illness**. It also relieves stress and tension and may contribute to a longer life.
3. Sport is a **social** activity that encourages the development of friendships. It can help people learn how to work and play together as part of a team.
4. Sport can satisfy, in an acceptable way, the **competitive** element that is inherent in most people.

Growth of sports participation

Know the PHEW factors that influence sports participation.

Just as people's leisure time has increased, so has their active involvement in sport. This is owing to a number of factors, often called the **PHEW** factors.

- **Peer pressure** – this is the influence that contemporaries have on each other. Individuals tend to be affected by group behaviour and if some of the group play sport, then others tend to take up sport as well. Also, individuals like to follow fashion, and to many people it is fashionable to play sport.
- **Home** – if parents play sport then they will introduce their children to sport and encourage their participation in sporting activities. They will also help their children with the cost of specialist equipment and clothing.

- **Education** – schools have to teach sporting activities to all children through the National Curriculum. This provides children with a range of sporting skills and, hopefully, stimulates a lifelong interest in sport. A good PE teacher can develop a positive attitude to the benefits of taking part in regular sporting activities.
- **Work** – more and more people are finding paid full-time or part-time employment in sport, and there is a large number of volunteers who give freely of their time to sport. Those who are paid might include coaches, instructors and trainers, as well as administrators. These people have to be qualified for the job that they do and they contribute to the increased participation in sport by the public at large. Many officials, such as judges, referees and umpires, work unpaid in sport but all are necessary if sport is to be made available to a large proportion of the population.

PROGRESS CHECK

1. What are the four main reasons why people take part in sport?
2. What are the PHEW factors that have contributed to the growth of sport?

1. It is fun, it contributes to good health, it is a social activity, it satisfies a competitive need.
2. Peer pressure, home, education, work.

8.3 Factors influencing an individual's participation

LEARNING SUMMARY

After completing this section you should be able to:

- *explain how various factors can influence participation*
- *give examples of each factor*

What are the factors that can influence our participation?

AQA A AQA B EDEXCEL OCR PE OCR G WJEC

Factors that affect an **individual's** participation in sport should not be confused with those that influence sport in a **general way**. Fig 8.2 shows those factors relating directly to the individual.

Fig 8.2 Influences on participation

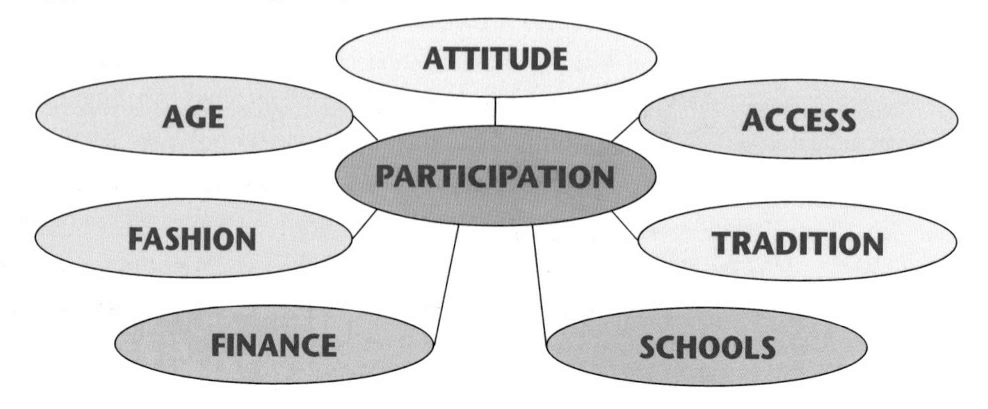

It is important to know these factors and how they influence participation.

Age

Age is a big influence on the amount of time that a person has to spend on sports participation (see Table 8.1).

Sport is not just for the young.

Table 8.1 Participation rates by age

Age range	Average participation in sport
Up to 16 years	steady rise, large amount of time spent
18 – 30 years	steady decline
30 – 50 years	steady rise, sometimes more time spent than by teenagers
50 plus	gradual decline

Fig 8.3 shows these changing trends in visual form.

Fig 8.3 Participation levels related to age

Know the ups and downs of sports participation.

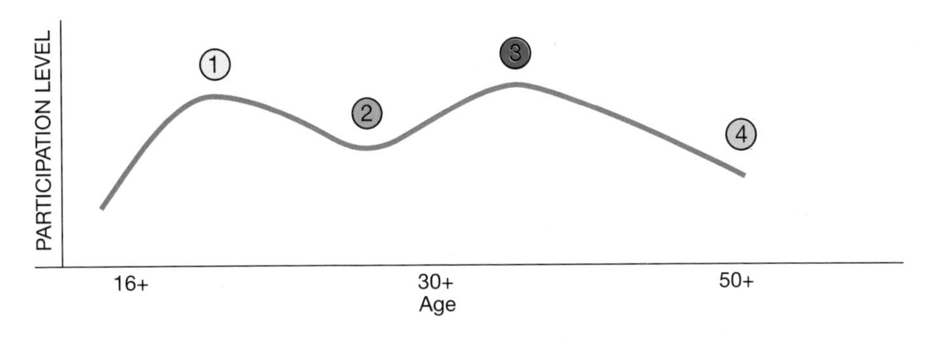

1. The first peak reflects that period when young people, as students, have time to play sport and tend to benefit from concessionary rates at leisure centres etc.
2. The first trough reflects the period when young people begin to spend more time and money on social activities, such as going out drinking and dancing with friends, and then on the establishment of family life.
3. The second peak reflects the period when the whole family can take part in sport together and then later as individuals.
4. The second trough reflects the period when people are getting older and are looking for less strenuous activities in life. This decline is more gradual than the first decline which develops rather quickly.

Attitude

Attitude is influenced, if not formed, by those most closely related to the individual.

Tradition influences attitudes.

Parents who are active in sport usually encourage their children to do the same. They generally expose their children to sporting traditions which will often be maintained in later life. This is not to say that children will always play the same sports as their parents, but they will have developed a sporting **ethos**.

Peer group acceptance is generally important to adults and children alike. The desire to join in with groups can be very strong. What our friends do, we want to do. If they have an interest in sport, then it is likely that we will want to be a part of that too. The advantage of this is that by joining one group of friends in sport, we are likely to meet and make friends with others who are also interested in sport.

Play sport early in life and you will probably play sport all your life!

Youth **clubs** and specific sports clubs make the young especially welcome. Club leaders hope that early participation in sport will help both the social and physical development of young children and will foster a future sporting tradition.

Access

The amount of time that can be spent on a sport depends to a large extent on the amount of sporting provision that is available locally. Schools tend to be well catered for but this is not always the case for the general public. However, more and more local authorities are providing **leisure and sports centres** that cater for individual and team activities. These are often open all day, seven days a week, meaning that those in employment can benefit from their provision. To encourage disadvantaged groups, local sports centres often provide concession cards for those on low incomes and crèche facilities for mothers with young children.

Some centres cater for single sports; most cater for a wide range.

Today, the vast majority of the population has access to sports facilities and few groups face restrictions. This has changed in the last 30 or 40 years; in the past **women** were often denied the chance to take part in those sports which were considered 'unsuitable' – the 'considering' probably being done by men. Fortunately, there has been a shift in this attitude and now an increasing number of sports is available to all.

Fashion

Fashion has influenced, and no doubt will continue to influence, sports participation. The fun-running boom started in the early 1980s and was fostered by local and national fun runs and city marathons. These events still take place today, with people running for fun and sometimes for charity, as well as for their own good.

A later development has been the rise in popularity of **aerobics**, and especially that of step aerobics. This fashion has caused an increase in female participation rates and has grown alongside the promotion of celebrity fitness videos. These encourage mainly women to look good, as well as feel good.

Aerobics is not a 'female' sport – it is just that few men try to do it.

An often-underrated influence in the field of fashion has been the **clothing industry**. This industry has changed dramatically in its approach to **sportswear**. Sports clothing is no longer just functional; it has to make a '**fashion statement**'. It still has to do the job properly, but it also has to look good on the wearer. New materials and bright colours reflect the mood of the participants as they enjoy their sporting activities.

Finance

Lack of funds should not stop you participating but it may govern where you participate.

Money is probably the major ruling factor in sports participation. In general terms, if an individual cannot pay, then he or she cannot play. This is certainly true with regard to privately run facilities, such as some golf clubs, fishing clubs and health clubs. However, local authority provision is more sympathetic to those in difficult financial circumstances. **Concessionary rates** are often available for the young, the non-working or senior citizens: those who tend to be on a low or fixed income. **Governing bodies** often promote their sports at subsidised rates.

Be aware of who can provide funds in sport.

The costs associated with the provision of facilities are now often met by a range of bodies, not just the user. Local authorities, the Sports Council, the National Lottery and industry (through **sponsorship**) all contribute towards the cost of sporting projects.

Schools

Do not forget the National Curriculum.

Education plays a great part in our lives. As children and young people, we have to go to school. We also have to take part in sport or physical education. If this is well taught, the foundations for enjoying a sporting life will have been established. School sport should provide the confidence that is needed to take part in a range of sporting activities.

Traditions

Areas are proud of their sporting traditions and try to maintain them.

Traditions come from the area where we grow up and live. They often develop over many years, reflecting the attitudes of specific communities and the geography of an area.

Up until a few years ago, the North of England was seen as the hotbed of rugby league, and there were few opportunities to get involved in the sport elsewhere in the country. Wales was considered to be a rugby union stronghold and Yorkshire a cricketing county.

In the past, sports often reflected the social class of the communities of the area. Working-class communities were more likely to support soccer teams and rugby league, while rugby union was often seen as an upper-class sport. Country sports such as golf, riding and hunting were also associated with the upper classes. Coastal areas have a strong tradition of water sports, while mountainous regions have seen climbing and hill walking flourish. Lakeland areas support inland sailing and fell walking.

However, the changes in attitudes to sports have, to some extent, broken down the traditional geographical and social distinctions related to a large number of activities.

1. Give reasons for the decline in sports participation in the 18 – 30 age group.
2. When did fun runs and city marathons first become popular in this country?
3. Give examples of how geography affects sports participation.

1. They spend more money and time on social activities, and the establishment of family life.
2. Early 1980s. 3. Coastal areas encourage water sports, mountainous areas encourage climbing, lakeland areas support sailing and fell walking.

Sample GCSE questions

1. Explain how age can be a factor which influences participation in sport.

As people get older their bodies slow down, deteriorate, become less efficient. Thus they participate less, or change to a less demanding sports activity. The very young are often physically undeveloped and so some activities are unsuitable, i.e. contact sports, BUT some activities are more suited to the young, i.e. gymnastics.

DO NOT concentrate on one age group only

[2]

2. Explain how education can be a factor which influences participation in physical recreation and sport.

All pupils must do PE and cover a range of activities. Many pupils experience extracurricular sport. Both of these can influence a pupil's attitude to sport. Good experience can encourage continued post-school participation.

When answering this type of question try to lead from school activities to post-school activities.

[2]

3. Explain how peer pressure can be a factor that influences teenagers' participation in sport.

Teenagers like to be accepted by those of a similar age. Teenagers like to mix with those of their own age. It is 'cool' to be part of the in-crowd and do what they do. These reasons reflect teenagers' general attitudes, as well as their attitudes towards sport. If some of a group take part, then so will others.

The link between general attitudes and sports attitudes is close.

[3]

4. State **three** notable and different reasons to account for people's participation in sport.

People participate in sport because:

- *they enjoy taking part*
- *they wish to maintain their health*
- *they find they are successful*
- *their family or friends take part*

Only three of these reasons are needed. The answer invites an essay type response, but bullet points will do.

[3]

NICCEA 1998 Paper 1 Q29 & 30, 1999 Paper 1 Q31 & 2000 Paper 1 Q37

Exam practice questions

(a) Explain how a local sports centre might provide for a number of groups from within the community.

....

....

....

....

....

.... **[6]**

(b) How can the following influence participation in sport?

(i) personal finance ....

....

(ii) tradition ....

.... **[4]**

(c) Give **three** reasons why leisure time has increased over the last 100 years.

....

....

.... **[6]**

(d) State **four** reasons why people participate in sport.

....

....

....

.... **[4]**

Major influences on participation

The following topics are covered in this chapter:

- *Social issues in sport*
- *Politics and sport*

9.1 Social issues related to participation

After completing this section, you should be able to:

- *explain the forms of discrimination that exist in sport*

Discrimination

The population of the United Kingdom originally developed from four major regional groups: the English, Irish, Scottish and Welsh. Over the last 50 years or so, two major ethnic groups, namely Afro-Caribbean and Asian, have been added to the population. These identities are influenced, in turn, by a range of religious beliefs, including the Roman Catholic, Muslim, Protestant and Jewish faiths. In addition, the sporting attitudes of our mixed heritage communities are also influenced by gender and disability.

In effect, the main causes of discrimination in Britain can often be traced to one or more of the following:

Remember the main causes of discrimination as GEDiR.

- **G**ender
- **E**thnicity
- **Di**sability
- **R**eligion

Gender

Traditionally, women did not have **equal opportunity** with men to participate in sporting activities. In the past this lack of opportunity reflected the views of many of the governing bodies of sport.

CCMM = Clothing + Class + Motherhood + Men

The four major reasons why women's participation in sport was originally held back were clothing, class, motherhood and men.

Clothing

There are many records of women taking part in a range of sports throughout the nineteenth century, although they were often hampered by the clothes that they wore (see Fig 9.1).

Fig 9.1 Ladies' hockey match, circa 1893 – clothes were restrictive

Before the advent of the bloomer, women tried to ride bicycles sidesaddle – not very successfully.

The first piece of ladies' clothing designed specifically for the then modern sportswoman was the culotte-style trousers pioneered by the American, **Fanny Bloomer**. These trousers, which became known as 'bloomers' or 'rationals', were designed with cycling in mind. This sport was a favourite of Queen Victoria and her royal patronage helped to promote cycling for women, though there is no evidence that the Queen ever wore a pair of fashionable bloomers.

At the turn of the last century all respectable women were expected to wear an undergarment called a **corset**. This tight-fitting piece of clothing, made of whalebone, severely restricted movement. In 1919, the international tennis star Suzanne Lenglen shocked Wimbledon by playing tennis without her corset. Her fast movement about the court helped her to many successes. Lenglen and other women of this period were, no doubt, also helped by the invention and popularisation of the **brassiere** in the 1920s. The development of less restrictive and more suitable sports clothing continued throughout the twentieth century and today women's sportswear is fashionable, practical and relevant to the event (see Photo 9.1).

Photo 9.1 Female dress to suit the activity – functional and smart

Class

Upper-class women had time for recreation, but lower-class women, the poor, did not.

Social class and the **status** of women generally in society have often dictated which sports they could participate in. In Victorian times, the working-class woman had little or no leisure time and, thus, could not participate in much sport. Middle and upper-class women were encouraged to play games such as badminton and lawn tennis, but only at a simple recreational level – their clothing would allow little running about (see Fig 9.2).

Fig 9.2 Women's tennis circa 1885

Wealthy women were expected to manage the home and servants, while working-class women had to work long hours. However, the two World Wars that took place in the twentieth century brought radical changes to the way all women lived and worked. The class distinctions began to be eroded. More women became independent of men as they were now employed. With their new-found leisure time they undertook a wider range of sporting activities.

Motherhood

Motherhood has always been a traditional role for women. In the past a woman was expected to be the homemaker and carer of the family, to look after the children and aged parents, acting as a 'housewife'. This traditional role persisted through a large part of the twentieth century. It is only recently that it has been widely accepted that women can combine the role of motherhood with other roles, including that of the sports performer.

KEY POINT **Mothers can play as much sport as women without children.**

Fanny Blankers-Koen won the 100 m hurdles at the 1948 Olympics. She was the mother of two children, and Mary Rand won gold in the long jump at the Tokyo Olympics shortly after giving birth to her daughter. There are now many women who successfully take part in a wide range of top-flight sports, while also fulfilling their roles as wives and mothers.

Campaigns are not always effective.

Although more women are taking part in a wider range of high-level sports, the number participating at grass-roots level has been slow to increase. The Sports Council's campaigns **Sport for All** in 1972 and **Come Alive** in 1977 promoted equal opportunity, but were not fully effective.

This Act still reflects out-dated male attitudes towards women and sport.

The **Sex Discrimination Act** of 1975 allows women to go to court if they feel that their rights are being abused – in sport as well as in the workplace. However, the Act makes the concession that 'when the physical strength or stamina of the average woman puts her at a disadvantage to the average man – as a competitor – then discrimination can take place.'

Unfortunately many sporting bodies use this clause to encourage the separate development of men's and women's sport.

Despite the obstacles, women are taking part in more and more sport. Notable female exponents of traditionally male sports are:

- Cheryl Robertson, a Commonwealth kick boxing champion and a mother of two children
- Jane Crouch, a world boxing champion since 1996
- Wendy Toms, the first woman to officiate at a Premier League Football match in 1997

Men

Women were never allowed to challenge male attitudes.

It can be said that men have contributed most to the slow development of women's sport. Women have been poorly catered for in the Modern Olympic games, mainly because men felt that most events were 'too strenuous for women'. Women were considered the weaker sex. Women were not allowed to compete in the 1500 m event until 1972 and the first women's marathon did not take place until 1984 at the Los Angeles Games.

Men always thought that they knew best, but they have been proved wrong in sport.

Men have consistently controlled the governing bodies of sports and promoted sport as a male activity. An example of this was the attitude adopted by the Football Association which refused to allow women's teams to affiliate to it and did not recognise the Women's Football Association (established in 1969) until 1993. Even today, boys and girls above the age of 11 are not allowed to play the game together.

Shirley Robertson beat the world's best yachtsmen to win gold at the Sydney Olympics.

Sports where men and women do compete on equal terms are sailing and equestrian events, such as show jumping and three-day eventing. In these events women have repeatedly proved that they are not only equal to, but often better than, their male counterparts.

Ethnicity

Traditionally, many sporting fixtures have been held among the UK's four home countries (England, Northern Ireland, Scotland and Wales). These have served to emphasise local and national pride.

KEY POINT

Birthplace and skin colour affect sports participation.

In the past, many sports discriminated against people because of their country of birth. If you were born in England, you played for England or nobody. This attitude has now changed and many sports allow a person to 'choose' their nationality through links with their parents' or grandparents' place of birth, or by fulfilling a residency qualification.

At a county level, discrimination also often existed. In some sports, a player could only play for the county where they were born. Things have changed, however. Some sports, such as **professional county cricket**, allow each home county to play up to two registered overseas players alongside British-born players.

At professional club level, overseas players were not always made welcome by the spectators and work permits, which they needed to allow them to play in the UK, were often refused. **Professional soccer**, however, has recently had to change its attitude towards overseas players. The 1995 **Bosnan Ruling** by the European Court effectively said that any player from any European Community (EC) country could play football for any club within the EC.

Although the number of non-white players in a wide range of sports has increased, some resentment towards these players is still evident. Soccer has had to implement the campaign '**Kick Race out of Soccer**' owing to the intolerant attitude of some groups of spectators. Non-white groups often feel that they are isolated within Britain and, thus, consider that they should support visiting teams playing against British sides. Whatever the causes, place of birth and colour of skin still affects the pleasure of participation in sports by a large number of individuals in Britain today.

Disability

Disabilities can be physical and sensory. Know the difference.

To some people, sport is for those who are fit and healthy. To many others, however, sport is for **all** and this includes those with a range of disabilities. In an effort to highlight some of the problems faced by disabled sportspersons, the United Nations nominated 1981 as the **International Year for Disabled People**. The aim was to encourage the provision of extra facilities for all disabled people in all walks of life.

The Sports Council supported this with the campaign '**Sport for All – Disabled People**'. This aimed to encourage the provision of suitable sports facilities for those with disabilities, as well as encouraging them to take part in sport. Today, no sports centre can be built without access ramps, changing and toilet facilities suitable for disabled people.

A wide range of events are competed in at the Paralympics. Great Britain won 41 golds at Sydney in 2000.

In 1948 Sir Ludwig Guttman founded the **Stoke Mandeville Games** for the Paralysed. These games started on the same day that the Olympic Games started in London and helped to show that sport was not just for the able-bodied. Eventually, a competition like the Olympic Games was organised for disabled sports people, timed to follow on after the main Games. Today these Games are called the Paralympics and they have a large following, as do the few events that are held for disabled people during the main programme of the Games.

Some disabled sportspersons strive to show that they should be judged by the same standards as their able-bodied colleagues. In 1982 Neroli Fairhall, a New Zealander who is confined to a wheelchair following a motor cycling accident, took part in the Commonwealth Games and won the gold medal for archery, shooting from her chair against able-bodied competitors. The picture below shows blind competitors competing in a recent half-marathon. The only concession asked is that they be led by a sighted person (see Photo 9.3). Photo 9.4 shows people who use wheelchairs competing in a similar event.

Photo 9.3 Blind runners competing in a marathon

Photo 9.4 Wheelchair competitors in a half-marathon

Religion

Be aware of the different religious beliefs followed in the UK.

At first sight it would seem discrimination on religious grounds has not been a feature of sport for many years. It is true that many of the top soccer clubs in the UK were founded as church boys' clubs. These were either Protestant or Catholic clubs and they would not accept players from the 'other faith'. Examples of this are Glasgow Rangers and Celtic, Liverpool and Everton. Today, such discrimination has largely disappeared. Even the Eire (Irish) Olympic boxing team is drawn from boxers of all faiths.

Some women who follow the Muslim faith are still restricted in the range of sports that they can participate in. Their religion dictates their dress code, which in turn can restrict participation. However, some attempts are being made to ease their integration into sport.

Some individuals cannot compete on a Sunday as they feel that this would go against their religious beliefs, and some largely Jewish football teams do not play games on Saturday, which is their Sabbath day.

1. List the four main causes of discrimination in Britain today.
2. How did Fanny Bloomer help to increase participation in cycling in the nineteenth century?
3. In which Olympic event have men and women always competed on equal terms?

1. Gender, ethnicity, disability, religion. 2. She invented culotte-style trousers, bloomers, for women. 3. Equestrian events.

9.2 Politics and sport

After completing this section, you should be able to:

- ***explain the effects that politics have had on sport***

Is it right to use sport for political gain?

NICCEA

Sports, like some wars, can bind a nation together. Sometimes a population will rally to support a national sporting team in world or international competition. This is one of the reasons why some governments have been prepared to use sport to further their own political philosophies. It is also the case that some sportsmen and women have used sport to highlight specific political ideals. Sport has been used by many to draw attention to a range of aspects other than sporting prowess.

KEY POINT

Sport and politics – should they be allowed to mix?

The Olympic Games has been used many times by various governments and individuals to try to prove a political point.

- **1936** – The Berlin Games were manipulated by the Nazi government of Germany to promote its own political ideals. These ideals included an attitude of extreme racial prejudice. Owing to Hitler's attitudes, he refused to acknowledge the successes of Jesse Owens, the black American athlete, who won four gold medals.
- **1956** – The Melbourne Games saw Spain and Holland withdraw in protest against the Russian invasion of Hungary. Communist China also withdrew, rather than compete against the nationalist Chinese of Taiwan.
- **1964** – At the Tokyo Games in Japan, the invitation to South Africa was withdrawn because of the latter country's policy of apartheid.
- **1968** – At the Mexico City Games, the invitation to South Africa was again withdrawn after much pressure from other African nations. Also, many black athletes from the USA chose to demonstrate against racial problems in their own country. They gave the black power salute on the winners' rostrum.
- **1972** – At the Munich Games, the team from Rhodesia (now Zimbabwe) was sent home after many black African nations objected to their participation, due to Rhodesia's treatment of its black citizens. The games were further disrupted when Arab nationalists invaded the Olympic village and killed several of the Israeli team.
- **1980** – The USA led a boycott of the Moscow Games as Russia had a poor record on human rights and had just invaded Afghanistan.
- **1984** – The Russians led a tit-for-tat boycott of the Los Angeles Games.

Be able to give examples of politics influencing national sports events.

In addition, many countries see the publication of the Olympic medal tables as an indication of their superiority over other nations.

Of a more long-lasting nature was the expulsion of South Africa from the Olympic and Commonwealth movements. They were expelled in 1970 following pressure from many African countries who objected to the political régime of South Africa. The **Gleneagles Agreement**, signed in 1977, reinforced this ban, but went on to say that countries should 'take every possible practical step to discourage sporting competition with South Africa – until the political situation in that country has changed'.

Only when the political policy of apartheid was changed were sporting links with South Africa re-established. This was direct use of sport to try to change the way an independent country governed itself.

1. Why did Spain and Holland withdraw from the 1956 Games?
2. Which team was sent home from the 1972 Games?
3. When was the Gleneagles Agreement signed and which country did it affect?

1. Because Russia had invaded Hungary. 2. Rhodesia, now called Zimbabwe. 3. 1977; South Africa.

Sample GCSE questions

1. Suggest **three** reasons why fewer teenage girls than teenage boys take part in sporting activities when they leave school.

any three from: religion, tradition, culture, available facilities

Be able to explain as well as list these.

[3]

2. 'Women participate less than men in sporting activities.'

(i) Give **three** reasons for this.

traditional attitude, lack of time, lack of money, lack of opportunity, children

(ii) Suggest **three** ways in which more women can be encouraged to take part in sporting activities.

better provision, women-only classes, reduction of costs, crèche facilities, a change in attitudes, encouragement of health and social aspects

A wide range of answers is possible but be specific and be able to explain those you select.

[6]

3. Explain fully how any **three** of the following can influence participation in sporting activities; family, class, school, fashion and age.

- *Family: parental involvement; parental interest in sport including paying for sport and being role models.*
- *Social class: fewer of the working class take part in sport; time and money; sport is seen as being for men, not women; not available to all classes; job can dictate amount of leisure time.*
- *School: good experiences will develop a positive interest in sport; education for leisure links school sport to clubs: wide range of sports taught.*
- *Fashion: some sports are in fashion; sportswear can be fashionable.*
- *Age: young have time but not money; older people have both time and money; schoolchildren 'switch off' when they leave school; young adults are housebound with children.*

Many of these answers relate to both sexes, not just women.

[6]

WJEC 1999 Paper 2 Q12 & 2000 Paper 2 Q12

Exam practice questions

(a) Explain how the Olympic Games have encouraged the development of sport for disabled people.

....

....

....

....

....

.... **[5]**

(b) Explain, with examples, how political and international problems have affected **three** of the Olympic Games since 1964.

....

....

....

....

....

....

....

....

....

....

....

....

....

.... **[15]**

The media and its influence on sport

The following topics are covered in this chapter:

- *Types of media*
- *Media presentation*
- *Effects of the media*

10.1 Types of media

After completing this section, you should be able to:

- *explain the written and the broadcast word*

Written and broadcast media

AQA A, OCR PE, OCR G

NICCEA

The media can be divided into two main areas:

- the **written** word
- the **broadcast** word (this includes television)

The written word

The written word includes:

- **newspapers**
- **magazines**
- **books**

These three types of written media report or comment on sport in some way. Whichever way they do it, the information they contain can be as much as 24 hours old, or more. Print media can never report immediately on sport, as TV can.

Newspapers

All newspapers contain substantial coverage of sporting features, usually on the back pages. Sports are reported, illustrations are often given, actions are commented on and opinions are expressed.

Many newspapers, especially regional ones, are not objective in their reporting.

Reports should be **factual** and **objective**, but this is not always the case. Some newspapers present a biased viewpoint: 'our side lost', not that the visiting opposition won. Often 'excuses' for losing are given.

Illustrations should reflect the action of the game, but this is not always so either. Pictures of males tend to show their skills in the game or reflect their efforts in performance. The pictorial coverage of women, however, is not always so objective. Photos may concentrate on what a woman is wearing or what she looks like. Sometimes the photographer even sets out to make a visual comment on the female form or to reveal the undergarments worn by a female player.

The actions of players, particularly those that can be sensationalised, regardless of whether they reflect the whole game, often take pride of place. Players' efforts can be underestimated and opinions may be expressed by those who have only a limited knowledge of the game. Such opinions are often based on supposition rather than fact. If newspapers are sometimes so lacking in professional objectivity, why do they put such effort into covering sports events?

KEY POINT

The reason for giving sports coverage is that sport helps to sell newspapers.

The fact that sport helps to sell papers is reflected in the range of sports covered. Soccer and racing in the winter, and cricket and racing in the summer are the main sports in many newspapers. Some do carry a wider range of sports, but few give equal coverage to the less popular sports or to women's sports.

Magazines

Sports-specific magazines tend to have more knowledgeable reporting and be more reliable.

Magazines cover a wide range of sporting activities and are often fully illustrated, but the news they carry can be over a week old. Most magazine coverage tends to be specialised: each publication relates to a specific sport. Because of this, a wide range of topics related to the sport can be covered and, more importantly, less popular sports often have their own weekly or monthly publication.

Books

Books come in a number of different styles. There is a wealth of autobiographical publications, especially written by celebrities from the more popular sports such as soccer, racing and rugby. Other books tend to be of an educational nature: they help people 'do a sport' or to obtain a qualification.

The broadcast word

This includes:

- **film** and **video**
- **radio** and **television**

Film and video

Films and videos, like magazines, can only present sport some time after it has taken place. The material is largely for entertainment or educational purposes.

Radio and television

Radio and television coverage, unlike that of film or video, can be instant. Play can be watched or heard as it happens, wherever it happens, around the world.

Much of the broadcast word is linked to sponsorship.

Instant replays can provide the basis for comments and analysis, whilst viewers and listeners can form their own opinions on live performances. The advent of many commercial television channels has increased the amount of sport shown and many of the less well-known sports are now getting more publicity.

1. What are the three main types of media using the written word?
2. What is the fundamental difference between the written word and the broadcast word?
3. Which part of the media allows you to form your own opinions of the sporting action and why?

1. Newspapers, magazines and books. 2. The written word can be 24 hours old: the broadcast word is mainly live. 3. The live broadcast, because you can see or hear it as it happens and can form your own opinions of the action.

10.2 Media presentation

After completing this section, you should be able to:

- ***explain the broadcasting rights related to sport***
- ***explain which sports are presented by the media***

Broadcasting rights

OCR G
WJEC
NICCEA

By selling rights, the event becomes a product, no longer just sport.

Broadcasting rights apply to television coverage of sporting events. In order to broadcast a sporting event, a television company must **purchase** the rights. The money is often paid to the governing body of the sport, but part or all may be paid to those competing. The Football Association (FA) may sell the rights to a football match and share the proceeds with the teams involved. Two boxers, however, could share the entire payment for coverage of a fight between them.

Once purchased, the rights may entitle a TV company to show the event once only, or as often as it wants. The TV company may sell on the rights to part of the event to other companies which may then show the highlights.

If a company buys **exclusive** rights, then only that company can broadcast the event.

Companies buy broadcasting rights to make money out of them, not to support the sport.

Some **satellite** TV companies have tried to buy up the rights to all the most interesting and exciting sporting events. Because these companies often charge viewers to see the event, they can afford to pay a higher price than the terrestrial companies, such as the BBC, which show events without specific charge, though in the case of the BBC there is the annual television licence fee.

There was a danger that all the 'best' matches and coverage of the most popular sports would be available only to those who could afford to pay extra to watch them. However, in 1996, the **Broadcasting Bill** was passed. This decreed that some sporting events should be made available to **all companies** so that any viewer could watch them. The events covered by the legislation include the **FA Cup Final**, the **Olympic Games**, the second week of **Wimbledon** and the **Grand National**. This was good news for those viewers who do not want to pay, but it could also deprive the events of a much-needed income.

Sports presented by the media

AQA A AQA B OCR PE OCR G WJEC NICCEA

Note that all these are male-orientated sports.

In the 1950s, before independent television (ITV) was fully established, the BBC broadcast only a limited number of sporting events. These included cricket, football and tennis. To counteract this monopoly, the developing ITV companies offered a different range of sporting events. These included horse racing, rugby league and wrestling – which became a national favourite in the 1960s and 1970s.

The controlling bodies of sport soon realised that television coverage of their sport meant that it would become more popular and that more people would participate in it. In turn, the more people who participated in a sport, the greater the population's interest in that sport and the greater the demand to see that sport on television.

KEY POINT

TV coverage makes sports popular.

Sports also look to make money out of TV companies.

Today, wherever possible, sports sell themselves to the highest bidder for a limited period only. With the growth of satellite and cable TV, there are more TV companies than ever before and many of these are looking to broadcast as much sport as possible, but as we have seen only a few get the chance to show the major events. This means that, with more and more time available to show sports, a wider range of sports is being broadcast. Certainly, a wide range of men's sports is shown, but most women's sports still do not get a large amount of air time.

1. What are broadcasting rights?
2. What types of sports are most often shown on television?
3. List two sporting events that are protected by the Broadcasting Act 1996.

1. Money paid by a media company to a National Governing Body or individuals for the right to broadcast a sport. 2. Mainly men's sports. 3. FA Cup Final, Olympic Games, second week of Wimbledon.

10.3 Effects of the media on sport

After completing this section, you should be able to:

- ***explain the positive effects that the media can have on sport***
- ***explain the negative effects that the media can have on sport***

Positive effects

AQA A AQA B OCR PE OCR G WJEC NICCEA

Of all the media, TV has the biggest impact on sport. The most important contribution that TV makes to sport is **money**.

Fig 10.1 Sports/TV loop

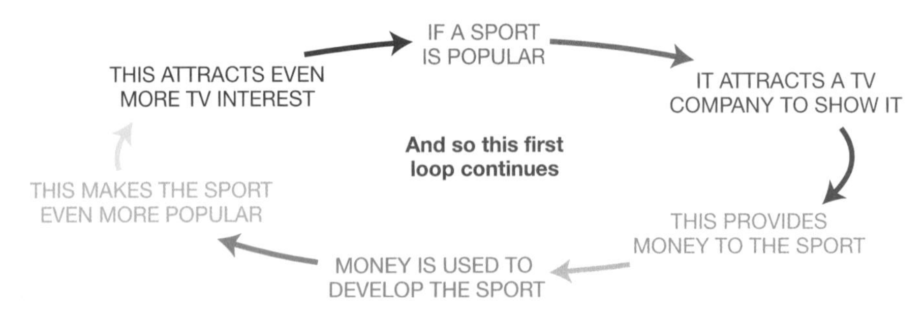

More TV cash = greater popularity.
With popularity comes a large slice of advertising revenue.

Fig 10.2 Sports popularity double loop

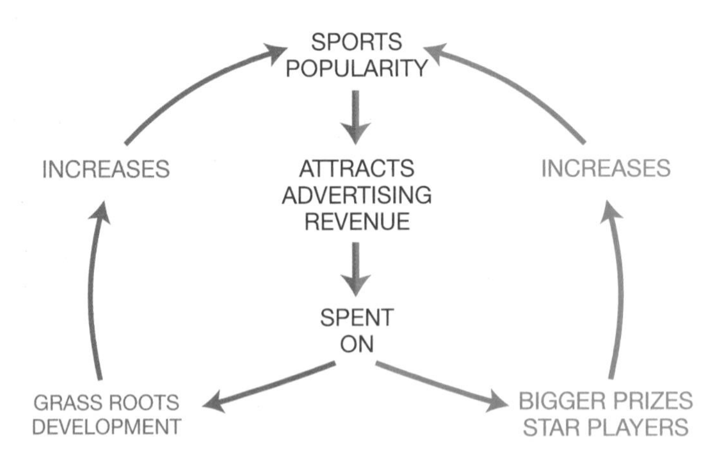

Some rules have changed because of media demands.

In addition to bringing cash to sport, television has also influenced the **rules** of some sports and the **times** that those sports are played (so that they can be broadcast live). For example, football can now be seen live throughout the week, which is an advantage to fans.

Some rules have been designed to increase the interest and excitement of a sport, and to bring about quicker results. This is shown clearly with the introduction of the **tiebreaker** rule in tennis. It speeds the game up, makes it easier to follow and generates more interest.

In addition, TV **educates** the viewers. They learn the rules of the sport from good commentary: greater understanding leads to more interest in the sport.

A spin-off from the increased wealth gained by TV coverage is that sports can provide better coaching and training for young players. This increases the overall standard of play in the sport and helps to create more interest in the sport.

Fig 10.3 Influences on sport of money generated by TV coverage

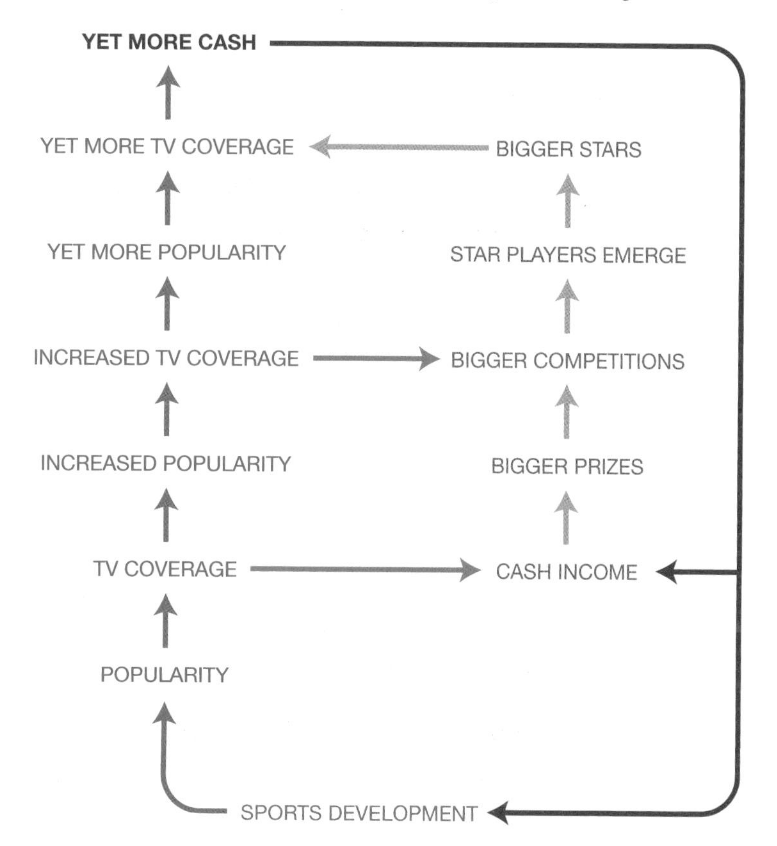

TV coverage gives players star status and this allows them to gain greater income from outside the sport. They do this by **product endorsement** and **sponsorship**, almost invariably of male-orientated products. So, most of the stars produced in this way are male sportsmen who can act as positive role models for younger players. Unfortunately, few women are accorded this status.

Negative effects

AQA A 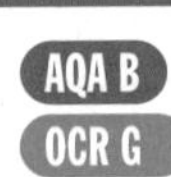 AQA B
 OCR PE OCR G
WJEC
 NICCEA

Just as the media contributes to the positive side of sport, it can also make **negative** contributions. Perhaps the biggest fault of the media is that is does not treat all sports equally. Some sports get lots of coverage, a great deal of money and, as we have seen, increased popularity. But what about those sports that are not shown on TV? They get no TV revenue and their popularity will probably never take off in a big way; in fact their following may be in danger of decreasing.

TV companies like to show sports that have established popularity.

It is suggested that extensive TV coverage means that spectators sit at home to watch sport, rather than paying at the turnstiles. Although this idea has some credibility, it fails to take into account how hard it is to get tickets to watch top-class sporting events, the fact that some fans may not be able to travel to a particular venue or the price of entry to some events. So, perhaps TV coverage does not affect live attendances after all.

On the positive side, we do see plenty of top-class performances. However, to boost viewing, TV companies want to see dramatic and sensational events. Head-to-head clashes between arch sporting rivals make good viewing, but some TV companies want to see them spiced up with personal conflicts. This can detract from the sporting ethic.

Some spectators love to hate some sports stars!

Stars are made by TV coverage: this can be good for the sport and helps to promote the game. However, some sections of the media do intrude on the personal lives of stars. They link their private lives to their public sporting achievements, often seeming to want to see the star fail in both arenas.

TV companies sometimes try to dictate to the governing bodies or organisers of a sport. They do this by forcing an event to take place at prime viewing time – to attract more TV viewers – rather than allowing it to take place at the best time for the event itself.

As we have seen, a sport needs TV coverage to increase its popularity and to make money to spend on development.

They also encourage sports to change their rules to fit in with TV time schedules. If a sport wants to get TV coverage, it must increase its suitability for a TV audience which is not always concerned with the skills of the sport. Why should female beach volleyball players have to wear skimpy costumes? If they do not, they will not get shown on TV and the sport will lose popularity. The costumes, however, do not increase the skill level in the game.

Sport makes money out of TV and TV makes money out of sport, but who gains most?

KEY POINT

TV needs sport, as it is popular with viewers. So TV will always buy broadcasting rights – but only on certain terms.

PROGRESS CHECK

1. In addition to cash, what is the other major benefit to sport of TV coverage?
2. What can TV coverage do for good sports players?
3. In what ways do TV companies dictate to sporting bodies?

1. Increased popularity. 2. Make them into stars. 3. Timing of events, rule changes, clothes to be worn.

Sample GCSE questions

1. Name **one** terrestrial television channel that shows sport.

BBC 1; BBC 2; ITV; Channel 4; Channel 5

[1]

2. Suggest **two** reasons why most sports shown on television are male-dominated sports.

- *Tradition - sport was always seen as a male preserve.*
- *Commercialism - male sports sell more goods.*
- *Role models - there are more male than female role models in sport.*
- *Spectacular performances - male sports are seen as more spectacular.*
- *Aesthetic - danger and thrills are wanted, not what looks good.*

Be specific and explicit in your answers.

[2]

3. *Rugby World* and *Athletics Weekly* are just two of the many specialist sports magazines published regularly. Suggest **three** reasons why magazines such as these are popular.

specific to the sport; cater for a specific target readership; tend to be up to date; contain a great deal of information about the sport; often are good sources of reference for the sport; give details of role models and stars of the sport

[3]

4. Using examples to help you, discuss in full both the positive and negative effects of television's coverage of sport.

Positive: shows new events, shows/uses new technology, gives good action replays, helps popularise sport, offers a wider coverage of sport, puts money into sport.

Negative: gives bad publicity, causes rule changes, controls time events are run, contradicts officials, can give negative influence, keeps spectators away.

Cover both aspects of the question and explain the points made.

[6]

WJEC 1999 Paper 2 Q14

Exam practice questions

(a) Give **one** reason why famous sportspersons are used to promote products in the media.

.... **[1]**

(b) Suggest **two** ways in which television affects sport.

....

.... **[2]**

(c) Suggest and discuss **three** ways in which the coverage of sport differs between the tabloid newspapers, e.g. *The Sun*, and broadsheet newspapers, e.g. *The Times*.

....

....

....

....

.... **[3]**

(d) 'Sport is presented in various ways on television, for example, live coverage of sporting events.' Discuss fully the ways in which sport is presented on television.

....

....

....

....

....

....

....

.... **[6]**

WJEC 2000 Paper 2 Q14

Organisation and provision of sport

The following topics are covered in this chapter:

- ***Structure of sport***
- ***Funding of sport***
- ***Providers of sport***

11.1 Structure of sport

LEARNING SUMMARY

After studying this section you should be able to:

- ***explain how sports clubs are organised at a local level***
- ***explain how sport is organised at a national level***
- ***explain how sport is organised at an international level***

Local organisation of sport

All sport is played by individuals. It is not essential to be a member of a sporting club if you want to take part in a sport. But it can be very useful, especially if you want to take part in competitions.

To take part in international competitions you must belong to a local sports club.

The pathway to representing your country is shown by the organisational structure outlined in Fig. 11.1.

Fig. 11.1 Organisational structure of competitive sport

INTERNATIONAL COMPETITIONS

NATIONAL COMPETITIONS

COUNTY COMPETITIONS

REGIONAL COMPETITIONS

CLUB COMPETITIONS

INDIVIDUALS

All local sports clubs have several things in common.

- They are run by the members.
- They are run for the members.

Know the functions of a sports club.

- They organise facilities.
- They organise competitions.
- They administer the paperwork of the club.
- They control the membership of the club.

Most local sports clubs have a similar structure:

- THE INDIVIDUAL MEMBER – the player

Know the duties of both members and officials.

- THE CLUB CAPTAIN – leads the players
- THE SECRETARY – deals with fixtures and correspondence
- THE TREASURER – deals with all matters relating to finance
- THE CHAIRMAN/PRESIDENT – leads and represents the club

When a player joins a club he or she takes on a responsibility towards the other players and those who organise the club, namely to play and support the club to the best of their ability. By the same token, the officers of the club (the secretary, treasurer and president) have a responsibility to the players to organise the club so that the individual can play the sport.

National organisation of sport

In order that their members can take part in competitions, local sports clubs need to have some sort of relationship with other clubs, either locally or nationally. Clubs usually achieve this by affiliating with the **National Governing Body** (**NGB**) of their sport.

Each sport in the UK has its own governing body, the functions of which are to:

Know the functions of NGBs.

- establish and maintain the rules of the sport
- organise competition in the sport
- promote the sport
- select international teams for the sport

Some governing bodies have been in existence for a long time; others developed recently (see Table 11.1).

Table 11.1 Establishment of some governing bodies of sport

Date	Club
1857	The Alpine Club
1871	The Rugby Football Union
1886	The Hockey Association
1949	The Basketball Association
1967	The British Orienteering Federation

To help promote their own and other sporting interests at a national level, the NGBs helped to set up the **Central Council for Physical Recreation** (**CCPR**).

The CCPR was established in 1935 with the express aim of representing the NGBs of sport. Today it acts as a voice for over 249 governing bodies. It is a voluntary organisation and is partly funded by the governing bodies.

The main aims of the CCPR are to:

You should know the aims of the CCPR.

- promote the development of sport and physical recreation
- give support to specialist sports bodies
- develop award schemes
- act as a consultative body to the various Sports Councils and others concerned with sport

KEY POINT
Overall, the CCPR serves the NGBs of sport and passes on their views to the Sports Councils, central government and local authorities.

Do not confuse the CCPR with the Sports Councils.

In addition to NGB funding, finance for the CCPR comes from donations, sponsorship and a grant from the **Sports Councils**.

The original Sports Council was established by Royal Charter in 1972 and was funded by an annual grant from central government. The aims of that Council were to ensure that:

- all young people had the opportunity to acquire sports skills and to take part in physical education
- all adults had the opportunity to take part in the sport of their choice
- everyone had the opportunity to improve their standard in sport
- the moral and ethical basis of sport was preserved and that sportspeople were safeguarded from political, commercial and financial exploitation whilst involved in sport

Be aware of this change in Sports Council organisation.

In 1996, however, the Sports Council was replaced by the **United Kingdom Sports Council (UKSC)**, together with separate sports councils for each of the home countries (England, Scotland, Wales and Northern Ireland).

The primary functions of the UKSC are to:

- improve the profile of sport in the UK
- give support to world-class performers at home
- promote standards of behaviour in sport, especially relating to drug-taking
- help promote national and international sporting events in this country

The sports councils of the separate home countries' aims are to:

Be aware of the different spheres of influence of each of the Sports Councils.

- help develop grassroots sport in that country
- improve the quality and amount of facilities available to sport
- provide services to support sporting excellence
- help in the distribution of National Lottery funding

KEY POINT
Sport England is the English Sports Council.

The English Sports Council, known as **Sport England**, is divided into 10 regions for administrative purposes and it manages five National Sports Centres (see Fig. 11.2).

Fig. 11.2 The 10 regions of Sport England and the national sports centres it manages

It is a good idea to know which person is the government Minister for Sport – the appointment changes from time to time.

In modern-day terms, the various sports councils are known as **quangos** (**Quasi-Autonomous Non-Governmental Organisations**). This means that, although they were set up by central government and are financed by central government, they are not controlled by central government. They get their grant from the Department of National Heritage, which is led by the Minister responsible for sport.

The sports councils and NGBs are supported in their work by a number of other bodies.

- **The Sports Aid Foundation** (**SAF**) – raises cash to assist those athletes who are in need of a grant to enable them to continue with their training. It raises finance from various sources, namely industry and commerce, sponsorship and the National Lottery.
- **The National Coaching Foundation** (**NCF**) – this was established to improve the expertise of coaches in all sports. There are several coaching centres throughout Britain which train coaches to teach sportspeople at all ability levels.

Be aware of the common interests of all these national bodies.

- **Disability Sport England** – this governing body aims to develop sport and recreation for people with disabilities. It also raises awareness of the success of international disabled sportsmen and women and aims to include these competitors in the conventional Olympic Games, as well as in Games organised especially for those with disabilities.
- **The Countryside Commission** (CC) – this was established in 1968 to look after the countryside. It advises on countryside issues, ensures that the countryside is available for recreational use and has set up the Country Code. Its areas of responsibility include the National Parks (see Fig. 11.3), long distance footpaths and bridleways.

Fig. 11.3 National Parks of England and Wales

International organisation of sport

KEY POINT **Home and international affairs are looked after by different bodies.**

Some organisations are directed specifically to the organisation of international sport.

- **The British Olympic Association** (**BOA**) – this organises the British Olympic team. The national governing bodies select individuals to join the team, but while competitors are abroad they are looked after by the BOA. The BOA also co-ordinates British bids to host the Games.

- **The International Olympic Committee (IOC)** – is the ultimate on all matters relating to the Olympic Games. Its membership is dra national Olympic committees and International Sports Federations.
- **The International Sports Federations (ISF)** – each ISF of a spo ultimate responsibility for all matters relating to that sport. Each nat governing body of a sport has representation on that sport's ISF (se Fig. 11.4).

Fig. 11.4 Administration of sport to international level

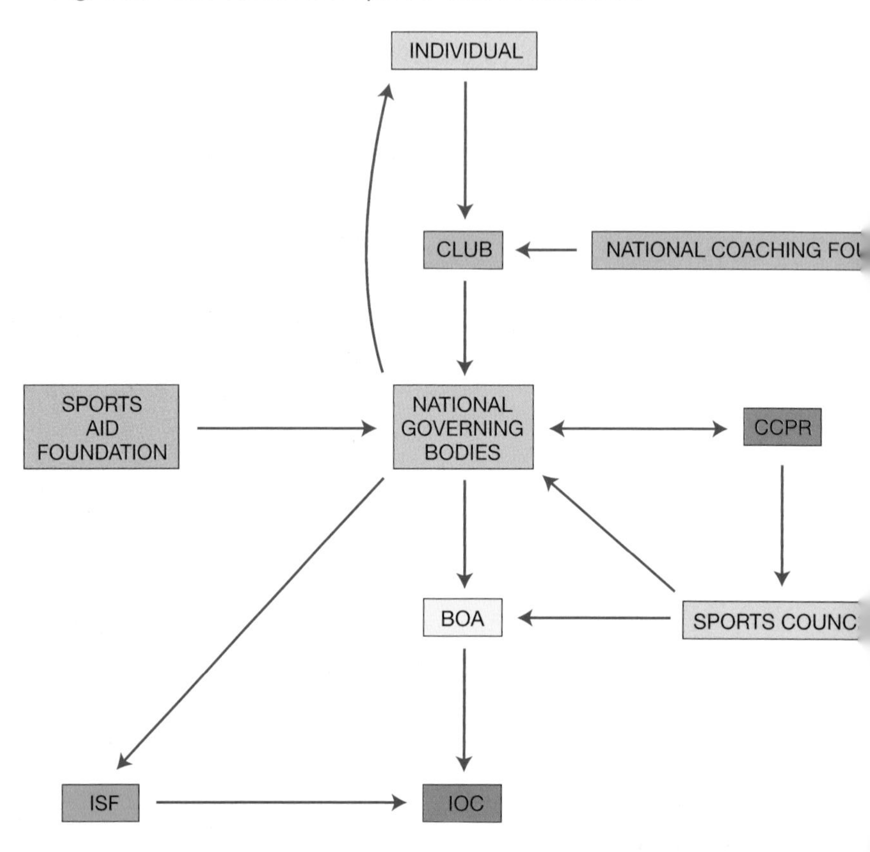

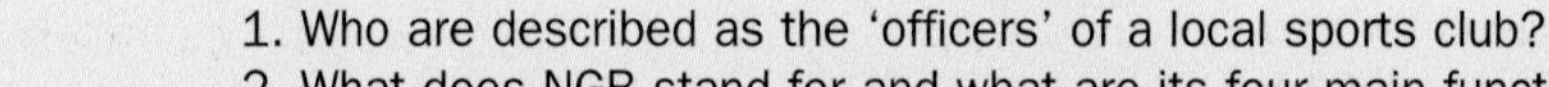

PROGRESS CHECK

1. Who are described as the 'officers' of a local sports club?
2. What does NGB stand for and what are its four main functions?
3. What are the main tasks of the UKSC?
4. What do the following stand for: SAF, IOC, BOA?

ent, secretary, treasurer. 2. National Governing Body; establish and maintain rules, competitions, promote the sport, select international teams. 3. Support world-class rs at home, promote standards of behaviour in sport, improve the influence of British oad, help promote national and international sporting events in this country. Aid Foundation, International Olympic Committee, British Olympic Association.

11.2 Funding of sport

After studying this section you should be able to:

- *describe how money is raised for sport*
- *describe the finance of amateur and professional clubs*

Raising money for sport

All sportspeople will be aware of the need to generate sums of money so that sporting activities can take place. There are several ways in which this money can be obtained.

- **Central Government** – the government does **not** put money **directly** into sport. However, it raises money through taxes paid directly by individuals and firms and indirectly through VAT on goods. From the revenue generated by taxes, it pays a grant (about £47 million a year) to the Sports Councils for them to spend on sport.

Central government does not own sports facilities or run sport – but it is an enabling influence.

- **Local Government** – local authorities raise their cash from council taxes on local residents and from business tax. All this income is spent on local services. Money is spent on local schools, youth clubs and sports clubs, and very often on the provision of leisure centres, football pitches in local parks and other sports facilities.
- **Gambling levies** – these are often the main source of income for smaller clubs. Most hold raffles to raise funds. On a much bigger scale, the government charges a levy on all gambling at the present time. In 2001 it took 12 pence of every pound spent on the National Lottery.
- **Private sector** – this type of finance comes in two specific ways:
  1. from developers who build private sports facilities and run them at a profit. Many fitness clubs, gyms and golf clubs operate this way.
  2. from private companies making loans to clubs in exchange for some franchise operation. Many breweries make loans to clubs who agree to sell only the breweries' products.
- **Sponsorship** – this provides money in several ways. Commerce, industry and local authorities are often prepared to invest in sport, a particular sports project or even an individual sportsperson. In exchange for a cash contribution, the sponsor's name is associated with the sport and is on permanent display.
- **Income** – the size of this must never be underestimated. Small clubs may charge fees for the use of their facilities, sell goods to their members or sell goods directly to the public. Some larger clubs, such as soccer clubs, obtain a huge income from selling sports merchandise and replica kits.

You should be able to explain the various sources that are available for funding sport.

- **Private individuals** – some very wealthy people like to invest sums of money in sports clubs. Some millionaires have bought their favourite football club, becoming chairmen. Both Bradford City and Blackburn Football Clubs are owned by wealthy men. Others just donate smaller sums of money to the club of their choice because of their love of the sport.

Financing amateur and professional clubs

AQA A AQA B OCR PE OCR G WJEC

Amateur clubs

KEY POINT **Amateur clubs have lots of sources of income, though most are small.**

Amateur sports clubs are run on quite small budgets. All the cash they get is spent on the members of the club.

Fig. 11.5 The amateur sports club wheel of wealth

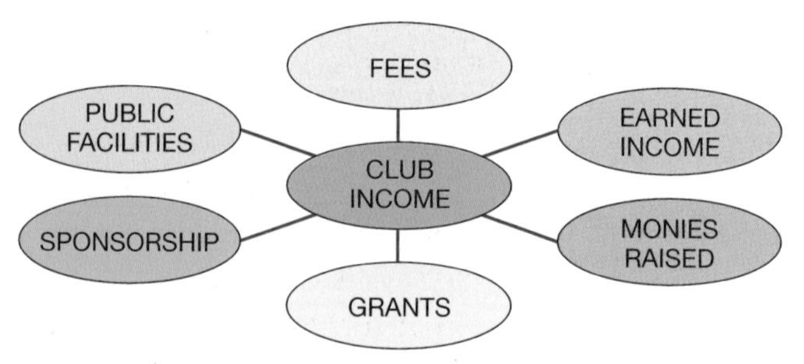

Be aware of the wide range of income sources.

- **Fees** – these form the basic income for some clubs. All club members are required to pay a membership fee. Players must pay more than social members, and youngsters pay less than adult members.
- **Earned income** – most clubs attempt to sell goods to their members and visitors. This merchandise could be kit, refreshments and items from the bar. If the club plays matches at a high enough standard, it may be able to charge admission fees to spectators. The selling of advertising space in match programmes and around the pitch can also provide a useful income. Clubs with their own facilities may rent out their club house for functions or use their ground to raise extra income from car boot or table top sales (see Photo 11.1).

Photo 11.1 A car boot sale at a rugby club in the off-season

- **Monies raised** – many clubs charge members match fees every time they play, to cover the cost of kit cleaning and repair. Most also organise raffles at specific times of the year and hold social events such as dinners and dances. These are expected to run at a profit for the club.
- **Grants** – these can form a large part of the income of a small club. They may be available from the local authorities to pay for regular expenses, or from the Sports Council or National Lottery for bigger projects (see Photo 11.2)

Photo 11.2 A voluntary club benefits from Lottery cash with the support of the Sports Council

- **Sponsorship** – this might come at a local level from small businesses who have an interest in the sport and may be restricted to the buying of kit with the sponsor's name on it.
- **Public facilities** – although not a form of income for a club, facilities are often provided either free of charge or at a reduced rate to local sports clubs. The clubs benefit by saving money. Local authorities often see this as providing a service to local people who are members of local clubs.

Professional clubs

Professional clubs often need to have a much greater income than amateur clubs, if they are to function properly. They have bigger outgoings than smaller clubs, especially as they have to pay wages to players and provide good facilities for spectators. They get their income from some similar and some different sources (see Fig 11.6).

Fig 11.6 The professional sports club wheel of fortune

Professional clubs are in business to make money.

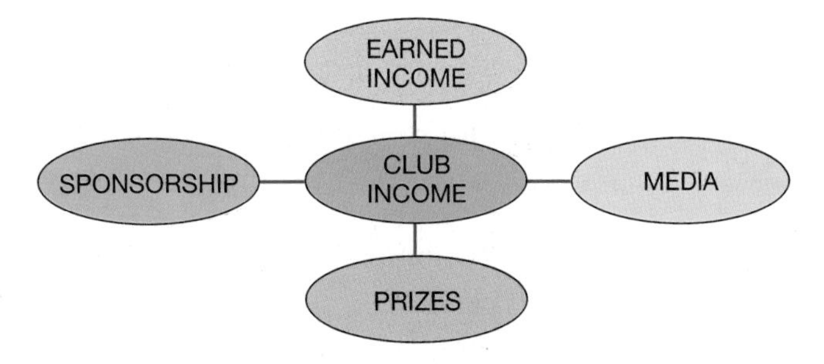

KEY POINT **Professional clubs may have fewer sources of income but each source generates a lot of money.**

Clubs change strips regularly to maintain income.

- **Earned income** – this is often quite extensive. Replica kits, sports merchandise, spectators' entry fees and advertising can all provide a large slice of income. The possible 'sale' of players also comes into this category.
- **Media** – media organisations often pay large amounts of money to broadcast matches. Some clubs have a regular contract either through their governing body or individually with radio or television, so that matches can be promoted and broadcast.
- **Prizes** – this source of income should not be overlooked. In professional sports circles not only can players earn large cash bonuses for winning popular competitions, but the clubs themselves may also receive large cash prizes.
- **Sponsorship** – this and the endorsement of goods provides a substantial income, especially for successful teams. Sponsors get a great deal out of sport: free advertising on players' strips and around the ground, an improved image and often lots of hospitality from the clubs. The negative side of this is that sponsors want to be associated only with the successful clubs, those that have a big following or those who get a large amount of media coverage. Loss of sponsorship cash can lead to less success on the pitch and a steady decline in support for the club.

PROGRESS CHECK

1. How does central government give money to sport?
2. Which popular gambling activity provides large amounts of cash for sport?
3. List three ways in which an amateur club and three ways in which a professional club might earn income from sport.

1. Through an annual grant to the Sports Council. 2. The National Lottery. 3. Amateur – selling goods, refreshments, renting out facilities, car boot sales; Professional – sports merchandise, replica kits, selling advertising space, entry fees from spectators, sale of players.

11.3 Providers of sport

LEARNING SUMMARY

After studying this section you should be able to:

- ***distinguish between private, public and voluntary provision***
- ***describe national and local providers of facilities***
- ***describe voluntary and commercial providers of facilities***

Modes of provision

AQA A AQA B OCR PE OCR G WJEC NICCEA

The provision of sporting facilities can be divided into three main areas:

1. **private**
2. **public**
3. **voluntary**

Private or commercial facilities

These clubs are provided by private companies for the benefit of those people who wish to **pay** to use them. Although they are often run on a membership basis, this membership has to be paid for and the profits from the club go, not to members, but to the owners. If these clubs do not get enough members to pay for their use, then they soon go out of business. Examples of this type of private club are health centres, hotel swimming pools and holiday centres, such as Centre Parcs and Haven.

Do not overlook sports facilities in the holiday industry.

Public or local facilities

As their name suggests, these facilities are provided from the **public purse** and are open to all members of the public. A membership scheme may exist, but it is never restrictive; anybody can join. The main providers of public facilities are local councils which develop facilities for the benefit of the community as a whole. They do not have to run at a profit, but should not run at a substantial loss either. Examples of this type of facility are local sports centres, leisure centres and swimming pools.

Local councils see local provision as part of their civic duty.

Voluntary facilities

These facilities are provided by groups of people within a local community. They usually provide for a limited number of sporting activities, sometimes only one. They have a membership scheme – members usually run the club – and any profits made go back to the membership to spend on the club. They usually own or lease their facilities and are organised by the members, for the members. Examples of this type of provider are local football, cricket and rugby clubs, the YHA and even yoga classes that take place in the local church hall. Individuals are not restricted in their use of these facilities; they are all available to everybody (see Fig. 11.7).

These are usually small local clubs that have links with NGBs.

KEY POINT **All sports provision comes from one of the private, public or voluntary sectors.**

Fig. 11.7 Providers of sports facilities

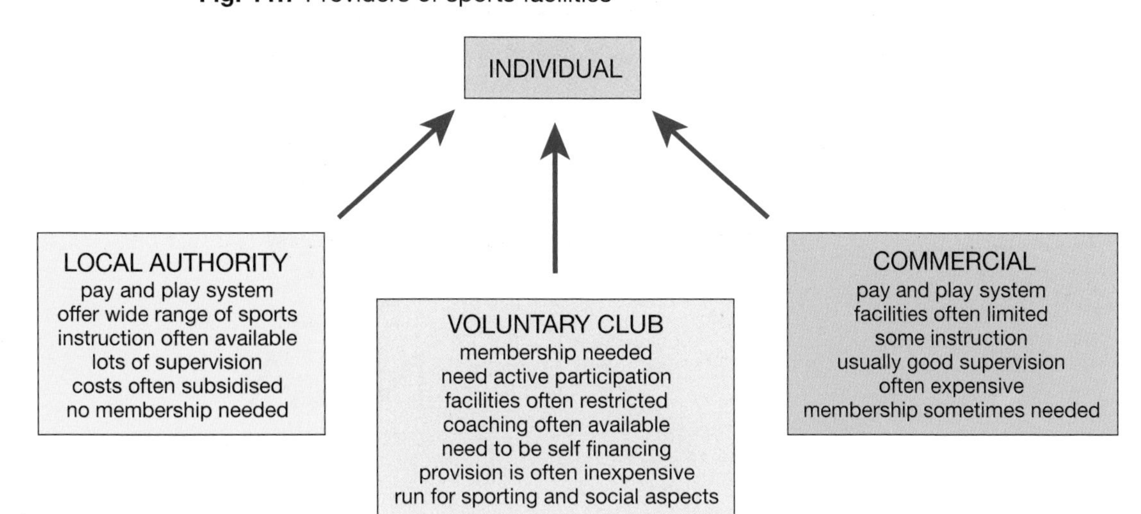

National and local providers

AQA A AQA B OCR PE OCR G WJEC NICCEA

The main providers of sport facilities on a national level are the Sports Councils, National Governing Bodies and a number of specialist organisations, such as the Countryside Commission, the Forestry Commission and the National Rivers Authority. The English Sports Council (Sport England) owns and runs five national sports centres, each of which concentrates on certain sports (see Fig. 11.2 and Table 11.2).

You should know these venues and the main sports they cater for.

Table 11.2 National sports centres run by Sport England

Venue	Location	Main sports catered for
Bisham Abbey	Buckinghamshire	tennis, soccer, hockey, squash, golf, weight training
Crystal Palace	London	athletics, swimming, judo, basketball
Lilleshall	Shropshire	soccer, table tennis, cricket, gymnastics, archery, hockey, golf
Holme Pierrepont	Nottinghamshire	water-based sports
Manchester	Lancashire	cycling

These centres often run national and international events, as well as providing top-class training and coaching facilities.

You should know about the contribution made by these national organisations.

- The **Countryside Commission** (**CC**) is a national organisation which provides local facilities, such as country walks and bridleways for public use and is responsible for the designation of **National Parks** and **Areas of Outstanding Natural Beauty** (**AONBs**).
- The **Forestry Commission** (**FC**) manages over 3 million acres of forest land to which the public has access for walking and riding.
- The **National Rivers Authority** (**NRA**) not only controls fishing on inland waterways, but also caters for canoeing, boating, water skiing and white water rapid rafting.

Fig. 11.8 Logos of CC, FC and NRA

Be able to quote the definition given by your Board.

You should know what your local authority provides for sport.

As we have seen, the main providers of facilities at a local level are **local councils** and **voluntary clubs**. Most local authorities have a department that is responsible for sport and leisure facilities – the Sports or Leisure Department – which works closely with other departments. It may work with a Parks Department which maintains the pitches, and an Engineering Department which maintains heating plant in a swimming pool. Sports and leisure complexes are expensive facilities to build and run, and often a local authority will develop such a facility in partnership with local industry and its national sports council (see Photo 11.3).

Photo 11.3 Sport and leisure facilities provided (note the Sport England logo, bottom left)

It is essential that these large facilities include a wide range of sporting opportunities. They must offer both indoor and outdoor sports, together with changing facilities for all types of user, whether they are the very young, the most active or those with a disability. Indoor pool, sports hall, squash courts and outdoor fields provide for sporting activities, but a centre may also cater for the leisure activities of the community. Halls can be used for concerts, displays and social events, and outdoor permanent play areas can be provided. To ensure the full use of these centres, adequate parking and local transport provision must be made.

Photo 11.4 Recreational facilities for the very young

CCT is a combination of public and commercial provision.

Although the local authority may build a sports or leisure complex, it won't actually run it. Under present government legislation the running of centres has to be put out to **Compulsory Competitive Tendering** (**CCT**). This means that the council fixes the budgets and sets its requirements, and then private companies bid to run the centre. The company which can offer the best service runs the complex. Many local authorities insist these operators provide specific groups with a reduced rate or privileged admission charges. This ensures that groups such as the young or non-wage earners can make full use of a centre.

Voluntary and commercial providers

AQA A 

OCR G

NICCEA

Be able to describe what voluntary clubs are and say why they exist.

Voluntary providers

This category covers a range of clubs that all provide sporting opportunities at a local level. They cater for the wide range of sporting interests that can be found in any local community. Many of these clubs hire their facilities from the local authority. Few athletics clubs can afford to acquire their own all-weather running track. Others, however, are more fortunate in that they have and run their own premises. Very often such clubs get a regular financial grant from their local authority to help towards their running costs. The main aim of these voluntary sports clubs is not to make a profit, but to provide sporting opportunities for local people at both a competitive and a recreational level.

Commercial providers

Be able to differentiate among commercial providers, private clubs, businesses and employer provision.

These are of two main types.

1. Some **companies** provide facilities for their **employees** – these include large commercial organisations such as banks or government departments. Although these facilities are in the commercial provision category, it is **not** the aim of the provider to make a profit. Employees are often asked to make a small donation towards the running cost of such facilities, but the bulk of their cost is borne by the employer. The company is providing a private facility for its employees. The main advantage of this type of provision is that employees, and often their guests, get sporting opportunities at a subsidised rate.
2. Some facilities are run on a **profit-making** basis – there is quite a wide range of this type of provision. Sport today is becoming a big industry and this is reflected in the growing number of private health clubs that have developed. Many of these only cater for specific sports and often charge large membership and entry fees. Only members and their guests can make use of them. Alongside these private clubs are enterprises such as fitness centres, bowling alleys and skating rinks.

Although most commercial providers are open to the public at large, like the private members' clubs, they exist to make a profit. Unless they make a profit, private sports clubs and other sporting ventures will close down.

1. What type of provider is (i) a local hockey club and (ii) a sports centre?
2. Which national sports centre provides for cricket, gymnastics and soccer?
3. What do AONB and CCT stand for?
4. Which type of commercial provider does not aim to make a profit?

1. Voluntary provider; (ii) public provider. 2. Lilleshall in Shropshire. 3. Areas of Outstanding Natural Beauty; Compulsory Competitive Tendering. 4. Private facilities provided by companies for their employees.

Sample GCSE questions

1. Give **four** ways in which money is raised for sport through gambling.

National Lottery, National Lottery Instants, football pools, betting levies on dog/horse racing, raffles, sweepstakes

[4]

Only four examples are required, but be clear and specific in your answer.

2. Explain how amateur sports clubs are funded.

Membership fees - most clubs charge a yearly rate for membership.

Earned income - sale of kit, refreshments; bar takings; admission charges; car boot sales; sale of advertising space round pitch.

Grants - small grants from a local authority and larger ones from the Sports Council/National Lottery.

Sponsorship - usually from local business rather than national concerns.

Monies raised by raffles and social events - usually organised at specific times of the year, e.g. Christmas, Easter, summer.

[8]

A list is not enough – an explanation is essential.

3. Explain how sponsors benefit from sponsorship deals.

Free advertising - name is put in front of many spectators and TV viewers.

Improved status - winning teams suggest that goods advertised are also winners, also that the goods have helped the team to win.

Hospitality - free tickets to big games so that the sponsors can 'show off' to clients.

Improved image - by putting money into a charitable event, a company can appear to be caring rather than purely commercial.

Scholarships - colleges and universities get top-class sports players who can bring sporting credit to the institution.

[8]

An explanation for each item on the list is necessary.

Exam practice questions

(a) Explain how a local authority might help a local sports club financially.

....

....

.... **[4]**

(b) Explain what grants might be available for developing amateur sports stars.

....

....

....

.... **[6]**

(c) Explain how and why the 'private sector' might finance sport.

....

....

....

.... **[5]**

(d) Explain the terms private, public and voluntary provision. Give **one** example of each type of provision.

....

....

....

....

....

....

....

.... **[10]**

Chapter

12 Centre-assessed components

In addition to the practical activities assessed under the 'A' and 'B' schemes of the AQA Board, a further **centre-assessed component** must be included by the candidate.

AQA A Centre-assessed component

AQA A

This takes the form of developing and performing an exercise/training programme. **This programme must relate to one of the practical activities you are being assessed in.**

Ten per cent of the final mark is allocated to this piece of work, so it is worth putting some effort into it.

This programme is assessed in **five** sections:

1	**Planning**	The ability to plan a programme that is appropriate to the activity and shows that you understand the principles of training.	20 marks
2	**Performing**	The ability to carry out the planned programme.	20 marks
3	**Monitoring**	The regular and accurate recording of results.	10 marks
4	**Evaluating**	An on-going and a summative appraisal of the programme.	20 marks
5	**Leading a warm up/ cool down**	The ability to design, lead and show understanding of a warm up/cool down.	10 marks

KEY POINT

This gives a total of 80 marks. An additional three marks can be awarded for good spelling, punctuation and grammar.

In the **Planning** section you must give the **aim** of your programme, show **awareness of relevant safety aspects**, use **appropriate exercise and skills** to improve techniques and relate your chosen exercises to **known training principles** such as progression/overload/frequency/duration.

In the **Performing** section you must **carry out** your programme, complete the exercises in a **safe manner**, show a **good attitude** towards your work and use **effective warm up/cool down** exercises.

In the **Monitoring** section you must provide brief notes on each session, **record** heart and recovery rates, put your results in **tabular form** and **summarise** your results at the end of each session.

In the **Evaluating** section you must **refer to pre-test scores**; assess the **appropriateness** of the exercises within the programme; and **refer to the principles of training**. You must comment on the **management** of the programme and the **enjoyment experienced** as you follow it; you must **identify and explain** any modifications made and **refer to the effects** of the programme. Comments should be made at the end of each training session. A **summative evaluation** at the end of the programme must also include reference to all the aspects already mentioned.

You must also **lead a warm up and cool down session** for a group of fellow students, using **suitable exercises** for your chosen activity. Emphasise **raising intensity**, **stretch exercises** and **mobility** work. During this activity, you will be assessed on the way you **organise** your group, how you use **your voice** and any **demonstrations** you give.

Sample programme A

AQA A

The following examples show how you might **begin** to plan a programme.

KEY POINT **In the planning and execution of your programme, follow the KIS (Keep It Simple) principle. Do not complicate matters.**

Circuit training for gymnastics

1 Planning

I want to improve my **flexibility** and **local muscular endurance** which are important fitness components for gymnastics.

I must establish my standard in the **sit and reach** and **shoulder flexibility** tests and the number of **press ups** and **sit ups** I can do in 30 seconds. I will construct a circuit that will concentrate on these aspects of my fitness.

Before taking part in each session I will follow a warm up and at the end I will complete a cool down. I will also check that all equipment is in a safe condition before starting.

I will start working at 50 per cent of my maximum on each activity, followed by a 15-second rest between activities. I will repeat the circuit three times each session and follow this programme three times a week. After every three sessions I will increase my target score by ten per cent. This will ensure that I am undergoing overload and maintaining progression throughout the programme.

2 Performing

My **flexibility** will be improved by the following warm up exercises:

- jogging for three minutes
- arm circles
- shoulder stretches
- hamstring stretches
- lunges
- sit and reach
- straddle sitting, chest to floor

All the stretching activities will be followed in an active manner for five to ten seconds. There should be a gradual **increase** of intensity as the warm up progresses.

My circuit for **local muscular endurance** will consist of:

- press ups
- star jumps
- squat thrusts
- sit ups
- dips
- shuttle runs

Try to include diagrams and/or pictures to show the circuit layout and the exercises you are doing.

My **flexibility** exercises (see above) will then be repeated to cool down.

For the cool down I will follow the same routine, but progressively **decrease** the intensity.

I will follow this programme three times a week for four weeks.

3 Monitoring

Before starting each session I will record my resting heart rate and at the end I will time myself to see how quickly it returns to normal.

Each session I will make notes on how I feel and how the work is going, and I will keep a progressive table of my heart rate data.

4 Evaluating

At the end of each session I will evaluate the work I have done and note any modifications I might want to implement in future sessions.

Remember to leave time to write up your rough notes neatly, ready for final submission.

On completion of the training programme I will retest myself using the same flexibility and local muscular endurance tests. I will then comment on any changes in my test results, how the programme has gone and how I felt as I was doing it.

Sample programme B

Running programme for hockey

1 Planning

The aim of the programme is to improve **aerobic fitness** and **speed**.

Hockey is a game that lasts for a long time and a high level of **stamina** is required. The game also requires players to **run short distances very quickly**, followed by work of lower intensity.

First of all, I will establish my aerobic capacity by completing the **Bleep Test**, then test my speed and agility by completing the **Illinois Agility Test**.

I will establish a suitable long distance running circuit that includes flat land, gentle slopes and short steep slopes. This will allow me to follow the **Fartlek** training concept.

Before taking part in each session I shall follow a suitable warm up, and at the end of each session I will perform a suitable cool down.

I shall complete the run, recording how long it takes me on each occasion and make a note of the weather conditions as these could affect my times.

I shall try to improve on my time for each run. This will ensure that I am following progressive overload during my training.

For safety's sake, I shall always try to run with a partner or let an adult know where I am running and what time I expect to get back.

2 Performing

Each training session will consist of a run over a prescribed outdoor course. The terrain will allow me to work for short periods of high intensity and longer periods of low intensity.

Before each session, I shall follow a set of warm up exercises:
- arm circles
- hamstring stretches
- lunges
- ankle and hip rotations
- jogging for five minutes

I shall follow all the stretching activities in an active manner for five to ten seconds, with a gradual increase of intensity as the warm up progresses.

For the cool down I will follow the same routine but progressively decrease the intensity.

3 Monitoring

Before starting each session I shall record my resting heart rate, and at the end of each session I will time myself to see how quickly it returns to normal.

I shall make notes on each session about how I feel and how the work is going, and I will keep a progressive table of my heart rate data.

4 Evaluating

At the end of each session, I shall evaluate the work I have done and note any modifications I might want to implement in future sessions. On completion of the training programme, I shall retest myself using the same tests.

I shall then comment on any changes in the test results, how the programme has gone and how I felt as I was doing it.

5 Leading a warm up and a cool down

You should:

- make a note of the exercises you intend to use on a small piece of card that you can keep in your pocket but refer to if necessary
- make sure that all the class are in front of you so that you can see them as they are working and they can see you
- make sure that they are working in a safe environment, not too close together
- explain slowly and clearly what you want the class to do, demonstrating difficult exercises
- start off with low level work and gradually build up the intensity
- concentrate on different parts of the body with each successive exercise
- follow the same routine for the cool down but in reverse, reducing intensity gradually

AQA Scheme B Centre-assessed component

AQA B

This takes the form of an Analytical Investigation

Twenty per cent of the final mark is allocated to this piece of work, so it is worth putting some effort into it.

The investigation is assessed in **five** sections:

1	**Audit**	Establishing current level of performance.	12 marks
2	**Planning**	How performance is to be improved.	12 marks
3	**Implementation**	Obtaining the evidence using the applied plan.	12 marks
4	**Analysis**	Using the evidence to demonstrate the effectiveness of the applied plan.	12 marks
5	**Evaluation**	A critical review of the whole process.	12 marks

A total of 60 marks can be awarded for this work with an additional three marks for good spelling, punctuation and grammar. Do not waste them.

In the **Audit** section, you must consider a particular sporting activity and make a well-informed choice as to which aspect of the performance to focus on.

In the **Planning** section you must clearly state the aim of your investigation. A well thought out, detailed plan must be produced that shows your understanding and the purpose of the investigation.

The **Implementation** section must show your extensive involvement in the investigation. Detailed observations must be recorded of all activities followed.

Remember the law of diminishing returns: very able people will not improve as much as less able performers over a short period of time, no matter how hard they work.

In the **Analysis** section, you must be able to show that you can draw conclusions in a competent and effective manner from the information you have recorded.

In the **Evaluation** section you must show clearly that you have met the original aims of your investigation. You must show how performance has improved, together with supporting evidence, and comment on the way the investigation has gone.

Sample topics

AQA B

The following topics, have been chosen as examples to show how the investigation might be tackled and presented.

In the planning and execution of your work try to follow the KIS (Keep It Simple) principle. Do not complicate matters.

Sample topic A

Investigation relating to the improvement of a specific skill for a designated sport.

1 Audit

- Video a golfer and observe his actions. Analyse his shots and record his major weaknesses.
- Decide which shots you would like to improve.
- Ensure that you have the expertise and resources to undertake such an investigation.

2 Planning

- State clearly your aim, e.g. to improve the chip shot.
- Research into the shot, e.g. to fully acquaint yourself with the skill of chipping in golf.
- Design some tests to establish the standard of your player.
- Design your training programme so that it is followed at least twice a week for six weeks.
- Include goal setting in your programme.

3 Implementation

- Construct suitable data collection sheets to record any scores and observations.
- Follow your training programme carefully.
- Observe your player carefully and record all progress made.
- Keep a record of scores so that targets can be set and adjusted.
- Re-test your performer at the end of the training period.

4 Analysis

- Consider the data you have collected and see if you can draw conclusions from it.
- Make sure that any interpretation that you make is fully supported by the evidence that you have collected.
- Present your analysis in a simple, clear manner.

Remember the law of diminishing returns: very able people will not improve as much as less able performers over a short period of time, no matter how hard they work.

5 Evaluation

- Show how you have met the aim of your investigation.
- Highlight the evidence that supports your claims.
- Critically evaluate your investigation, indicate how successful it was and identify any problems that you had to overcome as the investigation took place.

Sample Topic B

Programme leading to performance improvement in the long jump.

1 Audit

- Measure your standard in the long jump.
- Obtain a video recording of your performance in the long jump.
- Prepare data collection sheets to record your observations of your performance.
- Decide which phase of the long jump is most in need of improvement: run-up, take-off, flight or landing.
- Focus on those parts most in need of enhancement, e.g. run-up and take-off.

2 Planning

- Clearly state your aims: to improve the run-up and take-off phases of the long jump.
- Research the coaching techniques for this activity.
- Design a training programme to improve speed over short distances, e.g. a progressive shuttle run programme.
- Design a training programme to improve explosive leg strength, e.g. a plyometric exercise programme.
- Design the total programme so that it can be followed at least twice a week for six weeks.

3 Implementation

- Follow your training programme carefully.
- Record work you have done and modify it to suit your improvement.
- Set yourself attainable targets for speed and measurement of explosive leg strength.
- Record any data relating to performance.
- On completion of the programme re-test yourself over the long jump.

4 Analysis

- Consider the data you have collected and see if you can draw conclusions from it.
- Make sure that any interpretation you make is fully supported by the evidence you have collected.
- Present your analysis in a clear, simple manner.

5 Evaluation

- Show how you have met the aims of your investigation.
- Highlight the evidence that supports your claims.
- Critically evaluate your investigation, indicate how successful it was and identify any problems you had and how you overcame them.

These investigations are scheduled to take **six weeks**. Remember, however, that your schedule might suffer interruptions such as poor weather conditions or illness. Should anything like this happen, then you might have to extend the programme. It is doubtful if you would see much change in your performance in fewer than eight or ten training sessions.

Remember

- All practical physical training or improvement sessions must be preceded by a warm up and followed by a cool down. These should be related to your chosen activity and be described in your submission. You should also explain WHY you are doing warm ups and cool downs.
- Marks are given not only for planning and implementation, but also for analysis and evaluation. Analyse and evaluate each of your training sessions as well as giving a final summative evaluation at the end of your submission.
- If you use sources of information, credit them at the end.

Present your submission in five sections relating to the sections described at the start of this topic.

Exam practice answers

Chapter 1 The major body systems

(a) patella
(b) two from blood production, support, movement
(c) (i) closing of the joint
(ii) opening of the joint
(iii) circular movement combining flexion, extension, abduction and adduction

A diagram might help.

(d) a tough fibrous connective tissue joining two bones together: they strengthen and stabilise joints and limit movement in certain directions
(e) cardiac muscle – found only in the heart; smooth muscle – found in the bowel, bladder, blood vessels, intestines (also called involuntary muscle); skeletal muscle – found under the skin, attached to the bone, makes up the shape of the body (also called involuntary, striated or striped muscle)

Chapter 2 Fitness

(a) (i) time
(ii) frequency
(iii) type
(b) overload/progression
(c) progression
(d) reversibility
(e) specificity

Chapter 3 Training method and programmes

(a) one from: improves performance, improves fitness, improves skill, improves body shape, helps the 'feel good' factor
(b) (i and ii) two from the following, one for each part: based on running; periods of high level work; periods of low level work; variable speed; periods of rest/recovery; variable total time; variable distances; variable terrain
(c) (i, ii, and iii) three from the following, one for each part: wear appropriate clothing; be fit for the activity; warm up/cool down; build up gradually; handle equipment safely; follow the rules; use correct technique; work at an appropriate standard (within your known limitations)
(d) (i) types of injury should include: fractures, dislocation (hard tissue injuries); torn ligaments, torn cartilage, torn muscle, damaged tendons, inflammation of the joint, cuts and bruises (soft tissue injuries)

Cuts and bruises go together and are worth only one mark.

(ii) reasons for injury should include: impact with player/ground/equipment; rapid turning or twisting; sliding on hard/frozen ground; stress; overuse

Remember, the knee joint is a hinge joint. It is only meant to open and close in one direction: it is not designed to cope with stresses in other directions.

(e) (i) overload – involves putting the body under **progressively increased stress** in order to get a **training effect**

Remember, there are two parts to this explanation, both shown in red, and both should be mentioned.

Chapter 4 Skill

(a) A = agility; B = balance; C = co-ordination
(b) rotation
(c) (i) speed of response to stimuli
(ii) sprinter reacting to a gun, goalkeeper reacting to a shot: any example which illustrates 'fast response' will do

Chapter 5 Measurement in sport

(a) flexibility or suppleness
(b) any three from: identify strengths and weaknesses; get match/competition fit; indicate peaks of performance; motivation; help to plan training programmes; compare with previous performances; see if programme needs adjusting; give confidence to performer
(c) muscular strength – with a dynamometer
muscular endurance – bleep test, press ups, pull ups

Explain that the difference between the two types of test is the length of time taken when testing: strength uses a fast test, endurance uses a long-lasting test.

(d) Illinois agility run – this test measures speed and agility as a subject runs round cones placed in the shape of a letter T. The course is 10 m long and 4 m wide.

Only the essential parts of the test protocol have to be given; a diagram might help.

(e) any two from: it enables the player to change direction quickly; get away from a marker when in possession; avoid a marker

Only two facts are called for as only two marks are on offer.

Chapter 6 Factors affecting performance

(a) (i) vitamins
(ii) minerals
(iii) fibre/roughage
(iv) water
(b) (i) carbohydrates
(ii) carbohydrates/fats
(iii) fats
(iv) fats/carbohydrates
(c) (i) mesomorph
(ii) ectomorph
(iii) endomorph
(iv) ecto-mesomorph

This is a combination of two types.

Chapter 7 Sports related injuries

(a) one from: break, fracture, strain, torn ligament, torn tendon
(b) **R**est, **I**ce, **C**ompression, **E**levation

If you only give RICE you will not get full marks.

(c) check for any **D**anger; see if he can get any **R**esponse; check that the **A**irway is clear; check to see if there is any **B**reathing; check for a pulse to see if there is any **C**irculation
(d) Get help, if necessary by phoning 999

Chapter 8 Sport within society

(a) any three from:
concession entry – for those on low income, e.g. senior citizens and non-employed
restricted entry – women-only sessions, mother and toddler groups, late learners
minority provision – for less popular sports at peak times
crèche facilities – to encourage mothers back into participation
holiday courses – for young children when not at school

An explanation of each type of provision is required.

(b) (i) may restrict joining in an activity; may not be able to afford equipment for the activity; may not be able to afford the social aspects of the activity
(ii) may restrict provision for less popular sports; can demand an unfair share of time; may provide for a definitive part of the community only; can exclude minority groups

(c) any three from: increase in number of Bank Holidays; increase in number of paid holidays; shorter working week; shorter working life (people live longer in retirement, people start working later in life); more labour-saving goods (washing machines, dish washers); faster transport (easier to get to leisure facilities some distance away)

(d) any four from: enjoyment; get/keep fit and healthy; recover from illness; learn new skills; prepare for activity holidays; socialise; raise money for charities; win competitions/events

Chapter 9 Major influences on participation

(a) the incorporation of the Stoke Mandeville Games, first started in 1984, into the Olympic calendar; the promotion of athletic events as Olympic sports by the IOC; the recognition of categories of disability for Olympic events; separate Olympic Games for disabled athletes to follow straight after the main Olympic Games in the same host city; the inclusion of events for disabled people in the full Olympic Games as part of the recognised timetable

(b) any three from:
1972 Munich: terrorists massacre Israeli athletes
1976 Montreal: boycott by African nations as New Zealand was not excluded from the Games – N.Z. had earlier played S. Africa at rugby
1980 Moscow: political boycott by many western nations, led by the USA as Russia had invaded, and was at war with, Afghanistan
1984 Los Angeles: boycott led by Russia, claiming that Eastern bloc competitors would not be safe in America. In reality, this was a response to America's boycott of previous Games
1988 Seoul: friction between North and South Korea provoked a boycott by five countries, led by North Korea

In each case, 1 mark is awarded for date of Games, 1 mark for venue of Games and up to 3 marks for the explanation of the problem at each Games.

Chapter 10 The media and its influence on sport

(a) successful sportspeople promote the image that makes a product more successful in the market place; winners tend to be at the top of their sport; young, attractive and often articulate

(b) any two from: it promotes sport; it pays for broadcasting rights; wide coverage attracts sponsors; it can air issues relating to sport and coaching; it can force changes in the times that events are staged; it can encourage rule changes; it can encourage change in dress code

Both positive and negative effects can be offered for this answer.

(c) types of coverage:
tabloid press – covers smaller number of sports, usually the most popular; more given to sensationalism (private rather than sporting lives of personalities); reporting tends to be much more subjective
broadsheets – cover a wide range of sports; more objective in their reporting (less sensationalism); more factual; more editorial coverage; deeper coverage of sporting issues these factors can influence the image of sport, the popularity of the sport and the status of sports personalities/stars

List at least one item for each type of paper: you do not need every one of them.

You need to list the ways in which sport is covered and how these influence sport in order to get full marks for this section.

(d) methods of presentation: recorded coverage, recorded highlights, live coverage, results and information, news reports, documentaries, coaching programmes, educational programmes, fitness competitions, sports quizzes

In order to get full marks you must comment on the methods of presentation.

all these contribute to: popularising sport, keeping people up-to-date, generating interest, presentation of factual information

Chapter 11 Organisation and provision of sport

(a) local authority could provide: capital grants, pitches, changing facilities, club base, maintenance of pitches, sports development officers/coaches, free advertising

(b) local authority grants, Sports Aid Foundation, NGB grants, Sports Council grants, scholarships, sponsorship (either local or national)

(c) build facilities, run facilities through CCT; main object is to make money

(d) private – owned by commercial interests often for a private membership, e.g. a private golf club, a private health club, Centre Parcs
public – local authority provision for all, e.g. local leisure centre/swimming baths
voluntary – owned and run by the club members for themselves, e.g. local football or tennis club

Index

Index